DEDICATION

In memory of
Praya and Khunying Chavakij Banham

The Way It Is —

Ajahn Sumedho

For free distribution.

Publications from Amaravati are for free distribution. In most cases, this is made possible through offerings from individuals or groups, given specifically for the publication of Buddhist teachings. Further information is available from the address below.

Sabbadānaṁ dhammadānaṁ jināti
'The gift of Dhamma surpasses all other gifts.'

© Amaravati Publications, 1991

Amaravati Publications
Amaravati Buddhist Monastery
Great Gaddesden
Hemel Hempstead
Hertfordshire HP1 3BZ
England

ISBN 1 870205 11 1

CONTENTS

Photographs (and credits where known)

Page No.

Calligraphy: John Swain

Book design: Chris Millett Ven. Sucitto Karl Maslin

Sources of the text

The material in this book is taken from talks given by Ajahn Sumedho on the following occasions:

INTRODUCTION

This book contains a collection of teachings of Ajahn Sumedho given to people who are familiar with the conventions of Theravada Buddhism and have some experience of meditation. Most of the chapters are edited from talks either given during retreats for lay people or for Ajahn Sumedho's monastic (ordained) disciples, so they require some careful attention and are best read in sequence.

In the two - month monastic retreats Ajahn Sumedho develops a theme from the Buddha's teaching, linking it to other aspects of the Dhamma, embellishing it with accounts of his personal experiences, demonstrating its relevance to the society in general, or using it as an exhortation to the Sangha to live up to their aspiration of enlightenment. Although it is not possible to render the tonal depth and variety of these talks in a printed work, the mixture of short exhortations and pointers, longer contemplative reflections mingled with the chants that the monks and nuns have been reciting daily for years may suggest the atmosphere and scope within which the teachings are offered.

In many of these talks Ajahn Sumedho expounds on the uniquely Buddhist expression of 'not-self' (*anatta*). He maintains this to be the Buddha's way of pointing to the experience of Ultimate Reality that 'is the goal of many religions. During the monastic retreats, Ajahn Sumedho frequently teaches the Dependent Origination (*paticcasamuppada*) based on the approach of *anatta*. The Dependent Origination traces the process whereby suffering (*dukkha*) is compounded out of ignorance (*avijja*) and conversely suffering is eliminated (or rather not created) with the cessation of ignorance. Just as *anatta* – not-self – is the expression of Ultimate Truth, Ajahn Sumedho suggests that the root of ignorance is the illusion of 'Self'. He is trying not to annihilate or reject personal qualities but rather to point out how suffering (*dukkha*) arises through attempting to sustain an identity denoted by body and mind.

7

This *mistaken* identity is what the average person calls 'myself'. It can be detected in a latent state as self-consciousness, as a habitual mood of the mind such as conceit or self-criticism, or it can manifest as selfish bodily or verbal activity. The profundity of the Dependent Origination is that it describes how, even at its most passive, such wrong view creates habitual drives (*kamma*) and attitudes through which even a silent and well-intentioned meditator experiences suffering. *Kamma* ranges from the 'internal', psychological plane to the 'outer' realm of action. This habitual process then manifests in terms of body, speech or mind; all such manifestations being termed *sankhara*. Even moral action based on 'self-view' can lead to anxiety, doubt, 'sorrow, grief, pain, lamentation and despair'. Such is the meaning of the first 'link' of Dependent Origination '*avijja paccaya sankhara*' or 'dependent on ignorance are kammic formations'.

In its most complete formulation, Dependent Origination is expressed as:

'*avijjapaccaya sankhara; sankharapaccaya viññanam; viññanapaccaya namarupam; namarupapaccaya salayatanam; salayatanapaccaya phasso; phassapaccaya vedana; vedanapaccaya tanha; tanhapaccaya upadanam; upadanapaccaya bhavo; bhavapaccaya jati; jatipaccaya jaramaranam-soka-parideva-dukkha- domanassupayasa sambhavanti, evametassa kevalassa dukkhakhandhassa samudayo hoti.*'

This deals with arising of *dukkha*.

The cessation of *dukkha* is then mapped out:

'*avijjayatveva asesaviraga-nirodha sankharanirodho; sankharanirodha viññananirodho; viññananirodha namarupanirodho; namarupanirodha namarupanirodho; salayatananirodha phassanirodho; phassanirodha vedananirodho; vedananirodha tanhanirodho; tanhanirodha upadananirodho; upadananirodha bhavanirodho; bhavanirodha jatinirodho; jatinirodha jaramaranam-soka-parideva-dukkha-domanassupayasa nirujjhanti; evametassa kevalassa dukkhakhandhassa nirodho hoti.*'

In English this can be translated as:

> Dependent on ignorance are habitual formations; dependent on habitual (kamma-) formations is consciousness; dependent on consciousness are name-and-form (mentality-corporeality); dependent on name-and-form are the six sense-bases; dependent on the six sense-bases is contact; dependent on contact is feeling; dependent on

feeling is desire; dependent on desire is grasping; dependent on grasping is becoming; dependent on becoming is birth; dependent on birth is old age, sickness and death, sorrow, grief, lamentation, pain and despair.

Through the entire ceasing of this ignorance, habitual formations cease; through the ceasing of habitual formations, consciousness ceases; through the ceasing of consciousness, name-and-form cease; through the ceasing of name-and-form, the six sense - bases cease; through the ceasing of the six - sense bases, contact ceases; through the ceasing of contact, feeling ceases; through the ceasing of feeling, desire ceases; through the ceasing of desire, grasping ceases; through the ceasing of grasping, becoming ceases; through the ceasing of becoming, birth ceases; through the ceasing of birth, old age, sickness and death, sorrow, lamentation, pain, grief and despair come to cease. Thus is the ceasing of this whole mass of suffering.

There are many forms of dependence that are concerned in this analysis. It is helpful to remember that *paccaya* 'dependent on' or 'conditions' does not necessarily mean 'creates'. For example, one could say 'walking is dependent on legs' or 'ice is dependent on water' or 'catching the train is dependent on getting to the station at the right time' or even 'the view is dependent on the non-appearance of intervening objects'. Understanding this, the contemplative begins to realise that just as 'arising dependence' need not mean 'creation', the 'cessation' so valued by the Buddha need not mean 'annihilation'. In this lifetime, where Nibbana is to be realised, mentality-corporeality can 'cease' – i.e. the identification with physical and mental kamma-formations can cease so that life is no longer lived from the pleasure/pain principle dictated by the senses. (*nama-rupa-salayatana-phassa-vedana-tanha*). In this spirit, one could interpret the sequence in a more fluid way, for example :

> To the extent to which (*paccaya*) the mind has not comprehended (*avijja*) Truth, habitual drives (*sankhara*) manifest and condition (*paccaya*) awareness into a discriminative mode (*viññana*) that operates in terms of (*paccaya*) subject and object (*nama-rupa*) held (*paccaya*) to exist on either side of the six sense-doors (*salayatana*).

These sense-doors open dependent (*paccaya*) on contact (*phassa*) that can arouse (*paccaya*) varying degrees of feeling (*vedana*). Feeling stimulates (*paccaya*) desire (*tanha*) and, according to (*paccaya*) the power of desire, attention lingers (*upadana*) and so personal aims and obsessions develop (*bhava*) to give (*paccaya*) rise (*jati*) to self-consciousness. That self-consciousness, mental or physical, once arisen must follow (*paccaya*) the cycle of maturing and passing away (*jara-maranam*) with the resultant sense of sadness (*soka*) varying from sorrow (*parideva*) to depression (*domanassa*), to anguish (*dukkha*) and emotional breakdown (*upayasa*).

When the mind looks into the sense of loss and comprehends Truth (*avijja-nirodha*), habitual drives cease (*sankhara-nirodha*) and the awareness is no longer bound by their discrimination (*viññana-nirodha*); so that the separation of the subject and object is no longer held (*nama-rupa-nirodha*) and one does not feel trapped behind or pulled out through the six sense-doors (*salayatana-nirodha*). The sense-doors open for reflection, rather than being dependent on contact (*phassa-nirodha*) and impingement does not impress itself into the mind (*vedana-nirodha*). So there is freedom from desire (*tanha-nirodha*) and attention does not get stuck (*upadana-nirodha*) and grow into selfish motivations (*bhava-nirodha*) that center around and reinforce the ego (*jati-nirodha*). When no personal image is created, it can never bloat up, nor can it be destroyed (*jara-maranam-nirodha*). So there is nothing to lose, a sense of gladness, uplift, joy and serenity (*soka-parideva-dukkha-domanass- upayasa-nirodha*).

With the cessation of such a death-bound frame of reference there is the living of the True life, the Holy life, of which Ajahn Sumedho so evocatively speaks.

Although many of these talks were delivered to monastics, the beauty of the Dhamma is that it is available to those who wish to listen. It is with this in mind that this book is freely offered.

May all beings realise Truth,
Ven. Sucitto Bhikkhu.
Amaravati 1990.

'...Happiness forever'

... We have been meditating, watching our breath, contemplating the inhalation and the exhalation. We're using bare attention, mindfulness of the body while walking, standing, sitting and lying down. Rather than becoming fascinated, we're opening the mind to conditions as they are at the present time.

Notice how even in a beautiful place like this we can really make ourselves miserable. When we are here, we might want to be somewhere else; when we are walking, we might want to be sitting; when we are sitting, we might want to be walking. When we are meditating, we are thinking what we'll do after the retreat. Then after the retreat, we wish we were back here . . . hopeless, isn't it?

Before you came to this retreat, you were having problems at home and you were thinking, 'I can hardly wait till I go on retreat.' And then here you wish, 'I can hardly wait for the retreat to end.' Maybe you get very tranquil sitting there thinking, 'I want to be like this all the time,' or you try to get that blissful state you had yesterday but instead get more and more upset.

When you get these nice blissful states you grasp them; but then you have to get something to eat or do something. So you feel bad at losing the blissful state. Or maybe you haven't been getting any blissful states at all: just a lot of miserable memories and anger and frustrations arise. Everyone else is blissful; so *then* you feel upset because everybody else seems to be getting something from this retreat except you. . . .

This is how we begin to observe that everything changes. Then we have the possibility to observe how we create problems or attach to the good or create all kinds of complexities around the conditions of the moment; wanting something we don't have, wanting to keep something we have, wanting to get rid of something we have. This is the human problem of desire, isn't it? We're always looking for something else.

I remember as a child wanting a certain toy. I told my mother that if she got me that toy, I'd never want anything ever again. It would completely satisfy me. And I *believed* it – I wasn't telling her a lie; the only thing that was stopping me from being really happy then was that I didn't have the toy that I wanted. So my mother bought the toy and gave it to me. I managed to get some happiness out of it for maybe five minutes . . . and then I had to start wanting something *else*. So in getting what I wanted, I felt some gratification and happiness and then desire for something else arose. I remember this so vividly because at that young age, I really *believed* that if I got that toy that I wanted, I would be happy forever . . . only to realise that 'happiness forever' was an impossibility. . .

INVESTIGATING
THE MIND

The root of suffering is what we call *avijja* – not knowing, or ignorance of the way things really are. This basic ignorance is one of not understanding our true nature. We suffer because of views and opinions, and because of habits and conditions which we do not understand. We live our lives in a state of ignorance, not understanding the way things are.

If you listen to yourself very much, you can sometimes hear such statements as, 'I should do this but I shouldn't do that, I should be this way, I shouldn't be that way,' or that the world should be other than it is; our parents should be this way or that way and shouldn't be the way they are. So we have this particular verb tense ringing through our minds because we have an idea of what shouldn't be or should be. In meditation, listen to that opinion within yourself of what should be and what shouldn't be – just listen to it.

Our tendency is to try to become something; so we set a goal, create an ideal of what we would like to become. Maybe we think society should be other than it is. People should be kind, generous, unselfish, understanding and loving; there should be brotherhood; the government should have wise leaders and the world should be at peace. But the world is as it is at this moment in time and things are as they are. When we don't understand this then we are struggling. So listen inwardly to yourselves, to the constant crying, 'I am this way, I am not this way,' and penetrate this 'I am, I am not' with awareness.

We tend to just react and take it for granted that all the 'I am' and 'I am not' is the truth. We create ourselves as a personality and attach to our memories. We remember the things we've learned and what we've done – generally the more extreme things; we tend to forget more ordinary things. So if we do unkind, cruel, foolish things then we have unpleasant memories in our lives; we feel ashamed or guilty. If we do good or charitable things, then we have good memories in our lives. When we start reflecting on this, then we are going to be more careful about what we do and say; if we have lived life foolishly, acting on impulse out of desire for immediate gratification or out of an intention to hurt, cause disharmony or exploit others, our minds will be filled with very unpleasant memories. People who have led very selfish lives have to drink a lot or take drugs to keep themselves constantly occupied so that they don't have to look at the memories that come up in the mind.

In the awakening process of meditation, we are bringing awareness to the conditions of the mind here and now just by being aware of this sense of 'I am, I am not'. Contemplate the feelings of pain or pleasure – and any memories, thoughts and opinions – as impermanent, *anicca*. The characteristic of transiency is common to all conditions. How many of you spent the day really investigating this in every possible way while sitting, standing or lying down? Investigate what you see with your eye, hear with your ear, taste with your tongue, smell with your nose, feel and experience with your body and think with your mind.

The thought 'I am' is an impermanent condition. The thought 'I am not' is an impermanent condition. Thoughts, memories, consciousness of thinking, the body itself, our emotions – all conditions change. In the practice of meditation, we have to be quite serious, brave and courageous, to really investigate, to dare to look at even the most unpleasant conditions in life, rather than to seek escape in tranquillity or forget about everything. In *vipassana*, the practice is one of looking into suffering; it's a confrontation with ourselves, with what we think of ourselves, with our memories and our emotions, pleasant, unpleasant or indifferent. In other words, when these things arise and we are aware of suffering, rather than rejecting, repressing or ignoring it, we take the opportunity to examine it.

So suffering is our teacher. We have to learn the lesson by studying suffering itself. It always amazes me how some people think they never suffer. They think, 'I don't suffer. I don't know why Buddhists talk about suffering all the time. I feel wonderful, full of beauty and joy. I'm so happy all the time. I find life one fantastic experience, interesting, fascinating and a never-ending delight.' These people just tend to accept that side of life and reject the other because inevitably what delights us disappears and then we are sorry.

16

Our desire to be in a constant state of delight leads us into all kinds of problems, difficulties and situations. Suffering is not just because of massive things like having terminal cancer, or losing someone you love; suffering can occur around what is very ordinary, like the four postures of sitting, standing, walking, lying down. There's nothing extreme in that.

We contemplate the normal breath, and the ordinary consciousness. In order to understand existence, we contemplate ordinary feelings, memories and thoughts rather than grasp hold of fantastic ideas and thoughts to understand the extremes of existence. So we're not getting involved with speculation about the ultimate purpose of life, God, the devil, heaven and hell, what happens when we die or reincarnation. In Buddhist meditation you just observe the here and now. The birth and death that's going on here and now is the beginning and ending of the most ordinary things.

Contemplate beginning. When you think of birth you think of 'I was born', but that is the great birth of the body, which we can't remember. The ordinary birth of 'me' which we experience, in daily life is 'I want, I don't want, I like, I don't like.' That's a birth, or seeking to be happy. We contemplate the ordinary hell of our own anger, the anger that arises, the heat of the body, the aversion, the hatred we feel in the mind. We contemplate the ordinary heaven we experience, the happy states, the bliss, the lightness, the beauty in the here and now. Or just the dull state of mind, that kind of limbo, neither happy nor unhappy, but dull, bored and indifferent. In Buddhist meditation we watch these within ourselves.

We contemplate our own desire for power and control, to be in control of someone else, to become famous, or to become someone who is on top. How many of you, when you find out someone is more gifted than you are, want to put them down? This is jealousy. What we have to do in our meditation practice is see the ordinary jealousies, or the hatred we might feel for someone who might take advantage of us, or annoys us; the greed or lust we might feel for someone who attracts us. Our own mind is like a mirror which reflects the universe and you watch the reflection. Before, we would take these reflections for reality so that we became entranced, repelled or indifferent to them. But in *vipassana* we just observe that all these reflections are changing conditions. We begin to see them as objects rather than as a self, whereas when we're ignorant we tend to seek identity with them.

So in practice we are looking at the universe as it is being reflected in our minds. It does not matter what anyone else experiences; one meditator will sit here and experience all sorts of brilliant lights, colours, fascinating images, Buddhas, celestial beings – even smell wonderful odours, hear divine sounds – and think, 'What a wonderful meditation! Such brilliance came, such radiance! A divine being like an angel touched me and I felt this ecstasy. I've waited my whole life for this experience.' Meanwhile the next one is thinking, 'Why doesn't something like that ever happen to me. I sat for a whole hour in pain with an aching back, depressed, wanting to run away, wondering why on earth I'd come to this retreat anyway.' Another person might say, 'I can't stand all those people who have those silly ideas and fantasies. They disgust me; they just develop this terrible hatred and aversion in me. I hate the Buddha image sitting in the window. I want to smash it. I hate Buddhism and meditation!'

Now which of these three people is the good meditator? Compare the one who sees *devas* dancing in heaven, the one that is bored, indifferent and dull and the one full of hatred and aversion? *Devas* and angels dancing in the celestial realms are *anicca*, impermanent. Boredom is *anicca*, impermanent. Hatred and aversion is *anicca*, impermanent. So the good meditator, the one who is practising in the right way, is looking at the impermanent nature of these conditions.

When you talk to someone who sees *devas* and experiences bright lights, you start doubting your own practice and think, 'Maybe I am not capable of enlightenment. Maybe I am not meditating right.' Doubt itself is impermanent. Whatever arises passes away. So the good meditator is the one who sees the impermanent nature of bliss and ecstasy or experiences dullness, anger, hatred and aversion, and reflects on the impermanent nature of those qualities when sitting, walking or lying down.

What is your tendency? Are you very positive about everything? 'I like everybody here. I believe in the teachings of the Buddha, I believe in the Dhamma.' – That's a faith kind of mind. It believes, and that kind of mind can create and experience blissful things very quickly. You find that some of the farmers in Thailand, people who have hardly any worldly knowledge, who can hardly read and write, can sometimes experience blissful states, lights, *devas* and all that, and believe in them. When you believe in *devas*, you see them. When you believe in lights and celestial realms, you'll see them. You believe that Buddha is going to save you, Buddha will come and save you. What you believe in happens to you. If you believe in ghosts, fairies and elves, you find those things manifest for you. But they are still *anicca*, impermanent, transient and not-self.

Most people don't believe in fairies and *devas* and think such things are silly. This is the negative kind of mind, the one that's suspicious and doubtful and does not believe in anything. 'I don't believe in fairies and *devas*. I don't believe in any of that kind of thing. Ridiculous! Show me a fairy.' So the very suspicious and sceptical mind never sees such things.

There is faith; there is doubt. In Buddhist practice, we examine the belief and the doubt that we experience in our mind and we see that these two are conditions changing.

I have contemplated doubt itself as a sign. I'd ask myself a question like, 'Who am I?' and then I'd listen for the answer – something like, 'Sumedho Bhikkhu.' Then I'd think, 'That's not the answer; who are you really?' I'd see the struggle, the habitual reaction to find an answer to the question. But I would not accept any conceptual answer. 'Who is it sitting here? What is this? What's this here? Who is thinking anyway? What is it that thinks?' When a state of uncertainty or doubt would arise, I would just look at that uncertainty or doubt as a sign because the mind stops there and goes blank, and then emptiness arises.

I found it useful to empty the mind by asking myself unanswerable questions which would cause doubt to arise. Doubt is an impermanent condition. Form, the known, is impermanent; not knowing is impermanent. Some days I would go out and look at Nature and observe myself just standing here, looking at the ground. I'd ask myself, 'Is the ground separate from myself?' ' Who is that who sees the ground?' Are those leaves and the ground in my mind or outside my mind?' 'What is it that sees? Is it the eyeball?' If I took my eyeball out, would it be separated from myself? Would I still see those leaves? Are they still there when I'm not looking at them?' 'Who is the one that's conscious of this anyway?'

I also did some experiments with sound because the objects of sight have a certain solidity like this room – it seems fairly permanent, you know, for today at least. But sound is truly *anicca* – try to get hold of sound.

I investigated sound by asking, 'Can my eyes hear it? If I cut off my ears and ear drums, will there be any sound? Can I see and hear in exactly the same moment?' All sense organs and their objects are impermanent, changing conditions. Think right now, 'Where is your mother? Where is my mother?' If I think of her in her flat in California, it's a concept in the mind. Even if I think, 'California is over there', that's still the mind thinking 'over there'. 'Mother' is a concept, isn't it? So where is the mother right now? She is in the mind: when the word 'mother' comes up, you hear the word as a sound and it brings up a mental image or a memory or a feeling of like, dislike or indifference.

All concepts in the mind which we take for reality are to be investigated: know what concepts do to the mind. Notice the pleasure you get from thinking about certain concepts and the displeasure that others bring. You have prejudices and biases about race or nationality – these are all concepts or conceptional proliferations. Men have certain attitudes and biases about women, and women have certain attitudes and biases about men: this is just inherent in those identities.

But in meditation, 'female' is a concept and 'male' is a concept, a feeling, a perception in the mind. So in this practice of *vipassana*, we penetrate with insight into the nature of all conditions, coarse or refined. Insight breaks down the illusions that these concepts give us, the illusions that they are real. Conditions may arise; we can't stop the things that affect us in life – such as the weather, the economy, family problems, our background, our opportunity or lack of opportunity. But we can penetrate all these conditions – which are impermanent and not-self. This is the path of transcendence; transcending the mortal condition through awareness of the mortal condition.

The Buddha is the teacher, that within us which reminds us to observe the impermanent nature of all conditions and not to take any of them as reality. When we do, what happens? We have wars, strikes, battles and endless problems that exist in the world because ignorant beings take these conditions as reality. They attach to the mortal body as an identity. We get absorbed into these various symbols and concepts, and in that absorption we have to be born and die in those conditions. It's like getting attached to something that is moving, such as greed, and being pulled along by that movement. So we're born and die at that time. But when we don't attach any more then we're avoiding suffering from the movement and the limitations of changing conditions.

Now talking like this, people might question: 'How do you live in this society then, if it's all unreal?' The Buddha made a very clear distinction between conventional reality and ultimate reality. On the conventional level of existence we use conventions that bring harmony to ourself and to the society we live in. What kind of conventions bring harmony? Well, things like being good, being mindful, not doing things that cause disharmony, such as stealing, cheating and exploiting others; having respect and compassion for other beings, being observant, trying to help: all these conventions bring harmony.

So in the Buddhist teaching on the conventional level, we live in a way that supports doing good and refraining from doing evil with the body and speech. It's not as if we are rejecting the conventional world 'I want nothing to do with it because its an illusion' – that's *another* illusion. Thinking that the conventional world is an illusion is just another thought.

In our practice, we see that thought is thought, 'the world is an illusion' is a thought, 'the world is not an illusion' is a thought. But here and now, be aware that all we are conscious of is changing. Live mindfully, put effort and concentration into what you do, whether you're sitting, walking, lying down or working. Whether you're a man or a woman, a secretary, housewife or labourer or executive or whatever, apply effort and concentration. Do good and refrain from doing evil. This is how a Buddhist lives within the conventional forms of society. But they are no longer deluded by the body or the society, or the things that go on in the society, because a Buddhist is one who examines and investigates the universe by investigating their own body and mind.

✦

EVERYTHING THAT
ARISES PASSES AWAY

The Buddha said that the origin of all suffering is ignorance – so it's important to consider what he really meant by 'ignorance'. Most human beings in the world live very much as if they really are their habits, thoughts, feelings and memories. They don't take time or have the opportunity to look at their lives, to watch and consider how these conditions operate.

What is a condition? The body that we're with, the emotions and feelings, the perceptions of the mind, conceptions and consciousness through the senses – these are conditions. A condition is something that is added and compounded; something that arises and passes away; it's not the uncreated, unborn, unoriginated ultimate reality.

Religion is what human beings use to try to get back to that ultimate realisation beyond the cycles of birth and death, the supramundane wisdom or *lokuttara pañña*; Nirvana or Nibbana is the experience of that transcendent reality. This is when we suddenly know the truth, not by studying the Pali scriptures or a Zen book, but through direct experience.

We generally conceive the truth as being some *thing* and Nibbana as being some peaceful state of mind or ecstatic experience. All of us have experienced some kind of happiness so we like to conceive the Unborn, Uncreated, Unoriginated as a happy experience. But the Buddha was very careful never to describe the Ultimate Reality or Nibbana – he never said very much about it. People want to know what it is, write books on it and speculate about the nature of Nibbana – but this is exactly what the Buddha didn't do.

Instead, he pointed to direct knowing of conditions that change, that which we can know through our own experience at this moment. This is not a matter of believing anyone else. It's a matter of knowing at this present moment that whatever arises passes away.

So we put forth that kind of attention in our lives – to notice that whatever arises passes away; whatever condition of your mind or body – whether it is a sensation of pleasure or pain, feeling or memory, sight, sound, smell, taste or touch, inside or outside – it is just a condition.

It's important to reflect on the real meaning of 'ignorance' in the sense that the Buddha used it when he called it the origin of all suffering. 'Being ignorant' means that we identify with these conditions by regarding them as 'me' or 'mine' or as something that we don't want to be 'me' or 'mine'. We've got the idea that we've got to find some permanent pleasant condition, achieve something, get something we don't have. But we can notice that desire in the mind is a moving thing; it is looking *for* something, so it's a changing condition that arises and passes away – it's not-self. The expression 'not-self' (*anatta*) is not some kind of mantra* we use to get rid of things, but it is an actual penetration of the very nature of all desires.

As you look carefully, very patiently and humbly, you begin to see that the created arises out of the Uncreated and goes back to the Uncreated; it disappears and there is nothing left. If it was really you and really yours, it would stay, wouldn't it? If it was really yours where would it go – to some kind of storehouse of personality? But that concept and *whatever* you conceive is a condition that arises and passes away. Any time you try to conceive yourself, any concept or memory of yourself as this or that is only a condition of your mind. It's not what you are – you're not a condition of your mind. So, sorrow, despair, love and happiness are all conditions of mind and they are all not-self.

Notice in your life when you suffer or feel discontent – why? It's because of some attachment, some idea of yourself or someone else. Someone you love dies and you feel sorry for yourself; you think of the good times you've had and dwell on that, creating more conditions of mind. Maybe you feel guilty because you weren't giving or loving all of the time – that's a condition of mind also. You have a memory; you conceive of them as being alive – but that very idea of

---

* A word or phrase endowed with spiritual significance. It is used as a focus of attention and reflection by repeating it many times in meditation.

a person is a perception of mind – it's not a person, is it? Remember someone who is alive, who you wish you could be with right now – that's a condition of mind; or remember someone who's died, who you'll never see again – that's also a condition of mind.

Buddhist meditation is a way of looking at the conditions of mind, investigating and seeing what they are, rather than believing in them. People *want* to believe – when someone close to you has died, somebody has to tell you: 'Oh, they went up to heaven with God the Father, or they're living in the delights of Tusita heaven.' They say this so that you'll have a pleasant perception of mind – 'Well, now I know that my grandmother is happy up there in the heavenly realms, dancing with the angels.' Then somebody else says 'Well, you know, she did some pretty dreadful things, she's probably down in Hell, burning in the eternal fires!' So you start worrying that maybe you'll end up there too – but *that's* a perception of mind. Heaven and Hell are *conditioned* phenomena. So – if you reflect back to ten years ago . . . that's a condition of mind that arises and passes away, and the reason that it arises is because I've just suggested it to you. So that condition is dependent upon another condition, memory is what we have experienced, and the future is the unknown.

But who is it that knows the conditions of the moment? I can't find it: there's only the knowing, and knowing can know anything that is present now – pleasant or unpleasant – speculations about the future or reminiscences of the past – creations of yourself as this or that. You create yourself or the world you live in – so you can't really blame anyone else. If you do, it's because you're still ignorant. The One Who Knows we call 'Buddha' – but that doesn't mean that 'Buddha' is a condition. It's not to say that this Buddha-rupa knows anything; rather that 'Buddha' is the knowing. So Buddhist meditation is really *being* aware, rather than becoming Buddha.

The idea of becoming Buddha is based on conditions – you think you're someone who isn't Buddha right now, and in order to become Buddha, you have to read books to find out how to become one. Of course, this means that you have to work really hard to get rid of those qualities which are not Buddha-like; you are far from perfect, you get angry, greedy, doubtful and frightened, and of course, Buddhas don't have this – because Buddha is that which knows, so they know better. Then, in order to *become* Buddha you have to get rid of these unBuddha-like things and try to get Buddha-like qualities such as compassion and all these kinds of things. *And all these are creations of the mind!* So we create 'Buddhas' because we believe in the creations of the mind. But they aren't real Buddhas. They're only false Buddhas. They're not wisdom Buddhas, they're just conditions of our mind.

As long as you conceive of yourself as being somebody who has to do something in order to become something else, you still get caught in a trap, a condition of mind as being a self, and you never quite understand anything properly. No matter how many years you meditate, you never really understand the teaching; it will always be just off the mark. The direct way of seeing things *now* – that whatever arises passes away – doesn't mean that you are throwing anything away. It means that you're looking in a way that you've never bothered to look before. You're looking from a perspective of what's here and now rather than looking for something that's not here. So if you come into the Shrine Room thinking, 'I've got to spend this hour looking for the Buddha, trying to become something, trying to get rid of these bad thoughts, to sit and practise hard, try to become what I should become – so I'll sit here and try getting rid of things, try to get things, try to hold onto things' . . . with that attitude, meditation is a really strenuous effort and always a failure.

But if instead, you come into the Shrine Room and are just *aware* of the conditions of mind, you see in perspective the desire to become, to get rid of, to do something or the feeling that you can't do it; or that you're an expert, whatever – you begin to see that whatever you're experiencing is a changing condition and not 'self'. You're seeing a perspective of being Buddha, rather than doing something in order to become Buddha. When we talk about *sati*, mindfulness, this is what we mean.

I am really shocked and amazed at many religious people – Christians or Buddhists or whatever – who seem to be ignorant regarding the practice of their religion. Few people seem to have any perspective on religious doctrine and belief and disbelief. They don't bother to find out. They are still trying to describe the indescribable, limit the unlimited, know the unknowable, and not many look at the way they are. They believe what somebody else has told them.

Nowadays Theravada Buddhist monks will tell you that you can't get enlightened, there's no way you can even attain stream-entry, the first stage of sainthood – that those days are past. They believe that enlightenment is such a remote possibility that they don't even put forth much effort to see that all that arises passes away. So monks can spend lifetimes reading books and translating Suttas, still believing that enlightenment is impossible. But then what's the point of religion anyway? Why bother, if the ultimate truth is so remote, such an unlikely possibility? We just become like anthropologists, sociologists or philosophers discussing comparative religion.

Gotama the Buddha was one whose wisdom came from observing Nature, the conditions of mind and body. Now that's not impossible for any of us to do. We have minds and bodies; all we have to do is to watch them. It's not as if we have to have special powers to do that or that somehow this time is different from that of Gotama the Buddha. Time is an illusion caused by ignorance. People in the time of Gotama the Buddha were not any different from the way they are now – they had greed, hatred and delusion, egos, conceits and fears just like people nowadays. If you start thinking about Buddhist doctrines and different levels of attainment, you'll just get into a state of doubting. You don't have to check yourself with a list in a book – know for yourself until no condition of body or mind deludes you.

People say to me, 'I can't do all that. I'm just an ordinary person, a layman; when I think of doing all that, I realise I can't do it, it's too much for me.' I say, 'If you think about it, you can't do it; that's all. Don't think about it, just *do* it.' Thought only takes you to doubt. People who think about life can't do *anything*. If it's worth doing, *do it*. When you get depressed, learn from depression; when you get sick, learn from sickness; when you're happy, learn from happiness – these are all opportunities to learn in the world. Keep silently listening and watching as a way of life . . . then you begin to understand conditions. There's nothing to fear. There's nothing you have to get that you don't have. There's nothing to get rid of.

Saṅkhittena pañcupādānak·khandhā dukkhā
Seyyathīdaṁ
Rūpūpādānak·khando
Vedanūpādānak·khando
Saññūpādānak·khando
Saṅkhārūpādānak·khando
Viññāṇūpādānak·khando
Yesaṁ pariññāya
Dharamāno so bhagavā
Evaṁ bahulaṁ sāvake vineti
Evaṁ bhāgā ca panassa bhagavato sāvakesu anusāsanī bahulā pavattati
Rūpaṁ aniccaṁ
Vedanā aniccā
Saññā aniccā
Saṅkhārā aniccā
Viññāṇaṁ aniccaṁ
Rūpaṁ anattā
Vedanā anattā
Saññā anattā
Saṅkhārā anattā
Viññāṇaṁ anattā
Sabbe saṅkhārā aniccā
Sabbe dhammā anattāti
Te mayaṁ
Otiṇṇāmha·jātiyā jarāmaranena
Sokhehi paridevehi dukkhehi domanassehi upāyāsehi
Dukkhotiṇṇā dukkhaparetā
Appevanāmimassa kevalassa dukkhak·khandhassa antakiriyā
paññāyethāti

In brief, the five focuses of the grasping mind are dukkha.
These are as follows:
Attachment to form,
Attachment to feeling,
Attachment to perception,
Attachment to thinking,
Attachment to consciousness.
For the complete understanding of this,
The Blessed One, in his lifetime,
Frequently instructed his disciples in just this way.
In addition, he further instructed:
Form is impermanent,
Feeling is impermanent,
Perception is impermanent,
Thinking is impermanent,
Sense-consciousness is impermanent;
Form is not self,
Feeling is not self,
Perception is not self,
Thinking is not self,
Sense-consciousness is not self,
All conditions are transient,
There is no self in the created or the uncreated.
All of us
Are bound by birth, ageing and death,
By sorrow, lamentation, pain, grief and despair,
Bound by dukkha and obstructed by dukkha.
Let us all aspire to complete freedom from suffering.

THE FIVE KHANDHAS

As long as these human bodies are alive and their senses are operating, we have to be constantly on our guard, alert and mindful, because the force of habit to grasp the sensual world as a self is so strong. This is very strong conditioning in all of us. So the way the Buddha taught is the way of mindfulness and wise reflection. Rather than making metaphysical statements about your True Natures or Ultimate Reality, the Buddha's teaching points to the condition of grasping. That's the only thing that keeps us from enlightenment.

Buddha wisdom is an understanding of the way things are through observing oneself rather than just observing how the stars and planets operate. We don't go out looking at the trees and contemplating Nature as if it were an object of our vision: we actually observe Nature as it operates through this personal formation.

What we take ourselves to be can be classified as five aggregates or *khandhas*: *rupa*, form; *vedana*, feeling; *sañña*, perception; *sankhara*, mental formation or thought process and *viññana*, sense consciousness. These provide a skilful means of seeing all sensual phenomena in groups. The easiest to meditate on is *rupa khandha*, the form of the body, because we can sit here – it is stuck to the ground, heavy and it's a slower moving thing than mental phenomena (*vedana, sañña, sankhara* or *viññana*). We can actually reflect on our own body for long periods of time and meditate on the breath rather than on consciousness because breathing is something which we can concentrate on. Ordinary kinds of people can contemplate their own breath.

You can contemplate the feeling of your own eyes. They have sensations. Contemplate the tongue, the wetness of the mouth or your tongue touching the palate of your mouth. You can contemplate the body as a sense organ, giving you the sensations of pleasure and pain, heat and cold. Just observe what the feeling of cold or heat in the body is like; you can contemplate that because it is not what you *are*. It's an object you can see and easily observe as if it were something separate from you. If you don't do that, then you just tend to react. When you're too hot, you try to get cooler and take off your jumper. And then you get cold and you put it back on again. You can just react to those sensations of pleasure and pain in the body. Pleasure: 'Oh isn't that wonderful', try to hold onto that, have more pleasure. And the pain: 'Oh' – get rid of that; run away from anything uncomfortable or painful. But in meditation you can see these sensations. The body itself is a sensual condition that has pleasure, pain, heat and cold.

You can reflect on the forms that you see. Just look at something beautiful, like flowers. Flowers are probably the most beautiful things on the earth, and so we like flowers. So note when you look at a flower, how you're drawn to it, and want to keep looking at it: being attracted to what is pleasing to the eye. We can also look at something that is unpleasant to the eye – such as excrement. When you see excrement, cow dung on the path, you politely ignore it. Look at your own excrement. We produce it ourselves and yet it's something that we don't really want to go round showing other people. It's something we'd rather nobody ever saw us producing. We don't really feel drawn to go looking at it like we would at a flower. And yet we're quite willing to wear flowers, carry them around and keep them on our shrine.

It's not that you should find excrement attractive. I'm just pointing out that you can meditate on this force of the sensory world. It's a natural force. It's not bad or wrong but we can meditate on it in order to see our tendency to react to sensory experiences.

When you experience beautiful sounds or horrible ones, pleasant odours or stinking ones, pleasant tastes or unpleasant ones, pleasurable physical sensations or painful ones – meditate on these. See these things as they are: all *rupa* is impermanent. Beautiful flowers are only beautiful for a while; then they become repulsive. So we're observing this natural transformation from what is fresh and beautiful to what is old and ugly. Myself, I was a lot prettier when I was twenty. Now I'm old and ugly. An old human body is not very beautiful, is it? But it's the body, following what it's supposed to do. I'm glad it's not getting prettier. It would be embarrassing if it was.

Now the mental *khandhas* also operate on that same principle. *Vedana* is a mental state, the feeling you have of attraction and aversion around the physical things that you hear, see, smell, taste,

32

touch. The sensation of pain is just as it is, but then there's the reaction of liking or disliking – or just a movement toward or away from it.

You can be aware of feelings and moods. Note the heat that comes from anger and the dullness that comes from doubt or sloth-torpor. Note the feeling when you're jealous. You can witness that feeling. Watch jealousy instead of just trying to annihilate it. When jealousy conditions your mind out of aversion, rather than reacting to it or trying to get rid of it, you can begin to reflect upon it. When you're cold, what is coldness? Do you like it? Is feeling cold something terribly unpleasant or do you just make a lot out of it? What is hunger like? When you feel hungry, meditate on the physical feeling to which you tend to react by trying to get something to eat.

Meditate on the feeling of being alone or separate, or being looked down upon. If you feel that I don't like you – meditate on that feeling. And if *you* don't like me, meditate on that. Bring this into consciousness now; not analytically, trying to decide if your relationship to me is a dependent childlike relationship that you shouldn't have or getting caught up in Freudian psychology or whatever. But just observe the doubting uncertain state of mind in your relationships to others – and the feelings of confidence or lack of confidence, aversion or attraction that arise. These are *vedana*. We're all sensitive beings so there's a natural attraction and repulsion operating all the time. It's a condition in nature not a personal problem – unless we make it so.

Sañña khandha is the perception *khandha*. To grasp a perception means to believe in the way things appear in the present as permanent. That's how we tend to operate in our lives. So I might think, for example, 'Venerable Viradhammo is this way.' It's a perception I have whether I'm here, sitting next to Venerable Viradhammo or alone; whether he's helping me or angry with me. I have this fixed view. A fixed perception is not very conscious but I tend to operate from that particular fixed position if I believe in my perception. In that way, when I think of him, it's as if his personality is fixed and constant rather than being the way it is at this time. My perception of him is just a perception of the moment; it's not a soul that carries through time nor is it a fixed personality. So *sañña* is to be meditated on.

Sankhara are mental formations. We operate from these and from the perceptions of the mind, *sañña*. So the assumptions you have about yourself – from childhood, parents, teachers, friends, relatives and all that; whether you perceive yourself as good and positive or in a negative way or a confused way – it's all the *sañña/sankhara khandhas*.

You have memories or fears about what you might be lacking. You worry that there might be a serious flaw in your character or some repressed horrible desires lurking deep in your mind – which may arise in meditation and drive you crazy! *That* is another mental condition, that not knowing of what we are, so sometimes we imagine the worst possible things. But what we can know is that whatever we *believe* ourselves to be is a condition of the mind: it arises, it passes away and it is impermanent.

If we come from certain fixed perceptions of ourselves, then we conceive all kinds of things. If you operate from the position 'I am a man' and then become that perception of yourself, you never investigate that perception; you just *assume* and believe, 'I'm a man' and then conceive 'manhood' as being a certain way; 'what a man should be'. Then you compare yourself to what the ideal for manhood is and when you don't live up to those high standards of manhood, you worry. Something wrong! You start feeling upset or guilty or hating yourself because of the basic assumption that you are a man.

On a conventional level, this might be true; men are this way and women are that way. We're not denying the conventional reality, but we're no longer attaching to it as a personal quality, a fixed position to take at all times in all places. This is a way of freeing ourselves from the binding quality of the conditioned realm. If you believe yourself to be a man or a woman as your true identity and your soul, then that is always going to take you to a depressed state of mind.

All these are perceptions we have. We create so much misery over perceiving ourselves to be black or white or members of a certain nationality or class. In England, people suffer because of this perception of belonging to a certain class; in America we suffer from the perception that we're all the same, we're all equal. It's the attachment to any of these, even to the highest, most egalitarian perception, that takes us to despair.

Investigating these five 'heaps'*, aggregates or groups, you begin to see them. You can know them as objects because they're *anatta*,

---

*the literal meaning of *khandhas*

not-self. If you were these objects, then you would be unable to see them. You would only be able to *be* them, caught into them all the time without any ability to detach and observe them. But being men, women, monks, nuns, Italian, Danish, Swiss, English or American is only a relative truth, relative to certain situations.

Yet we operate our lives from fixed positions and identities. Throughout the world, we have national and racial prejudices. These are just perception and conception (*sañña/sankhara khandhas*) that we can observe.

When you have a fixed view about somebody – 'One thing I can't stand is Hondurans' – you can observe that in your mind, can't you? Even if you have strong prejudices and feelings and you try to get rid of them, that comes from assuming that you *shouldn't* have any prejudices or bad feelings towards anybody and you *should* be able to accept criticism with an equanimous mind and not feel angry or upset. That's another very idealistic assumption, isn't it? You see *that* as a condition of mind and keep observing.

Rather than hating ourselves or hating others for being prejudiced, we observe the very limitations of any prejudices or perceptions and conceptions of the mind. We meditate on the impermanent nature of perception. In other words, we try not to justify or get rid of or change anything but just to observe that all things change – all that begins ends.

Then we meditate on the *viññana khandha*, the sensory consciousness of the eye, ear, nose, tongue, body and mind. We are aware of the movements of consciousness of the senses. When we look at something or hear something – it changes very rapidly.

All these five *khandhas* are *anicca*, impermanent. When we chant: *rupam aniccam, vedana anicca, sañña anicca, sankhara anicca, viññanam aniccam*, this is very profound. Then: *sabbe sankhara anicca*. *Sankhara* means 'all conditioned phenomena', all sensory experience – the sense organs, the objects of the sense organs, the consciousness that arises on contact – all this is *sankhara* and is *anicca*. All is conditioned. So *sankhara* includes the other four: *rupa, vedana, sañña, viññana*.

With this you have a perspective from which the conditioned world is infinitely variable and complex. But where do you separate *sañña* from *sankhara* and *sankhara* from *viññana* and all that? It's best not to try to get precise divisions between these five aggregates;

they're just convenient means for looking at things, helping you to meditate on mental states, the physical world and the sensory world.

We're not trying to fix anything as this is permanently *sankhara* and that is definitely *sañña*, but to use these labels to observe that the sensory world – from the physical to the mental, from coarse to refined – is conditioned, and all conditioned phenomena are impermanent. Then we have a way of seeing the totality of the conditioned world as impermanent rather than getting involved in it all. In this practice of insight meditation, we're not trying to analyse the conditioned world, but to detach from it, to see it in perspective. This is when we really begin to comprehend anicca; to insightfully know sabbe sankhara anicca.

So any thoughts and beliefs you have are just conditions. But I'm not saying that you shouldn't believe in anything; I'm just pointing out a way to see things in perspective to avoid being deluded or to grasp the experience of emptiness or the Unconditioned as a personal attainment. Some of you have been grasping that one as a kind of personal attainment, haven't you? 'I know emptiness. I've realised emptiness' – patting yourselves on the back. That's not *sabbe dhamma anatta* – that's grasping the Unconditioned, making it into a condition; 'Me' and 'Mine'. When you start thinking of yourself as having realised emptiness, you can see that also as a condition of the mind.

Now *sabbe dhamma anatta*: all things are not-self, not a person, not a permanent soul, not a self of any sort. That's also very important to contemplate because *sabbe dhamma* includes all things; the conditioned phenomena of the sensory world *and* the Unconditioned, the Deathless.

Notice that Buddhists make no claim for Deathlessness as being a self either! 'I have an immortal soul' or 'God is my true nature!' The Buddha avoided such statements. Any attempt to conceive oneself as anything at all is an obstacle to enlightenment because you still attach to an idea, to a concept of self as being part of something. Maybe you think there's a piece of you, a little soul, that joins the bigger one at death. That is a conception of the mind that you can know. We're not saying it's untrue or false, but we're just being the knowing, knowing what can be known. We don't feel compelled to grasp that as a belief; we see it as only something that comes out of the mind, a condition of the mind, so we even let that go.

Keep that formula 'all conditions are impermanent, all things are not-self' for reflection. And then in your life as you live it, whatever happens, you can see *sabbe sankhara anicca, sabbe dhamma anatta*. It keeps you from being deluded by miraculous phenomena that might happen to you, and it is a way of understanding other religious conventions. Christians come along and say: 'Only through Jesus Christ can you be saved. You can't be saved through Buddhism. Buddha was only a man, but Jesus Christ was the son of God.' So you think, 'Oh, I wonder, maybe they're right.' After all when you go to one of these 'born again' meetings everybody's radiating happiness; their eyes are bright and they say, 'Praise the Lord!'

But when you go to a Buddhist monastery, you just sit there for hours on end watching your breath; you don't get high like that. You start doubting and you think, 'Maybe that's right; maybe Jesus is the way.' But what you can *know* is that there's a doubt. Look at that doubt or the feeling of being intimidated by or averse to other religions. What you can know is that these are perceptions of the mind: they come and go and change.

Keep a constant cool reflection on these things rather than trying to figure it out or feel that you have to justify your being a Buddhist. Christians start saying, 'You don't do anything for the third world,' and you say, 'We . . . we . . . we . . . chant! We share merit and we radiate loving-kindness.' This sounds weak in the face of malnutrition and starvation in Africa! But now there's this opportunity to understand our limits. All of us would definitely do something about starvation in Africa if we felt that there was something one individual could do at this time. Reflect upon this – what is the real problem? Is it starvation in Africa or is it human selfishness and ignorance? Isn't starvation in Africa the result of human greed, selfishness and stupidity?

Therefore, we open our minds to the Dhamma. We wisely reflect upon it and then realise it. Truth is to be realised and known within the context of personal experience. But the practice is a continuous one – after 25 years I still practise all the time. Things change: people praise and blame and the world goes on. One just keeps reflecting upon it with *sabbe sankhara anicca, sabbe dhamma anatta*. When you recognise the conditioned and the Unconditioned, then you can develop the Path without confusion.

The goal now is to realise Nibbana, the Deathless, or non-attachment – realise what it's like not to be attached to the five *khandhas*. Realise that when you're sitting here and you're really at peace. There's no attachment to the five *khandhas* then; but you might attach to your perception of that peacefulness and try to use your meditation in order to be peaceful again. That's why it's a continuous letting go rather than an attainment.

Sometimes, when you get calm on these retreats, you can have a very peaceful mind. And you attach: so then you meditate in order to attain that blissful state. But insight meditation means looking into the nature of things, of the five *khandhas*, seeing them as *anicca* – impermanent; as *dukkha* – unsatisfactory. None of these *khandhas* can give you any kind of permanent satisfaction. Their very nature is unsatisfactory and *anatta*.

Start to investigate and wisely consider *sabbe sankhara anicca, sabbe dhamma anatta* rather than holding on to what you perceive to be your attainment and resenting anybody that disturbs you. *Note* what is attachment. When your mind is really concentrated, let go of it. Rather than just indulging in that peaceful feeling, attach to something. Worry about something. Deliberately do it so that you begin to see how you go out and grasp things or worry about losing the feeling of peace.

As you begin to understand and experience letting go in your practice, you realise what Buddhas know: *sabbe sankhara anicca, sabbe dhamma anatta*. It's not just the words – even a parrot can say the words – but that's not an enlightened parrot, is it? Insight is different from conceptual knowledge. But now you're penetrating, going deep into this, breaking through the illusion of self as being anything at all or nothing: if you believe that you don't have a self – that's *another* belief; 'I believe I don't have a self.

The Buddha pointed to the way between these two extremes: of believing you have a self and believing that you don't have a self. There is nothing to be found in the five *khandhas* which has a permanent self or soul: things arise out of the Unconditioned and return to the Unconditioned. It is through letting go rather than through adopting any other attitude that we no longer attach to mortal conditions.

'...All the time in the world'

. . . As we sit here during this retreat, we have to pay attention to things that are not at all interesting. They may even be unpleasant and painful. To patiently endure things rather than to run off in search of something interesting is a good discipline, isn't it? It is good to be able to just endure the boredom, the pain, the anger, the greed – all these things – instead of always running away from them. . . . Patience is such an important virtue. If we have no patience, there is absolutely no possibility of getting enlightened. Be *extremely* patient. . . .

I used to like the kind of meditation where I could sit and get very calm – and then when pain would arise in the body, I'd want to get rid of it so that I could stay in that state of calm. Then I began to see that wanting to *get rid* of pain was a miserable state of mind. Sometimes we sit for several hours; sometimes all night long. You can run away from it, but after a while you begin to come to terms with physical pain. I've used practices like 'having all the time in the world.' rather than struggling to get rid of it so that I could come back to my 'real' meditation. I've learned to take time to be with the pains in my body if they come up in consciousness rather than trying to get some bliss.

Somehow, when I would say, 'I have all the time in the world, the rest of my life, to be with this pain,' it would stop the tendency to want to get rid of it. My mind would actually slow down for long periods of time without following or creating a desire. Some of you have this idea of *conquering* pain, getting over the 'pain threshold' – but that's a disaster. . . .

PRECEPTS

Tonight is the new moon* and so today we reaffirmed our commitment to *sila*: the Patimokkha for the bhikkhus, the ten precepts for the nuns and the eight precepts for the anagarikas. In reaffirming our commitment, we can take these eight precepts to a refined level of interpretation. So with the first precept – *panatipata veramani* – to refrain from killing other creatures – even though none of us may be prone to murder or physical violence, it is important to make it clear in our mind that our intention in this life is to not intentionally even *harm* others. Then the second precept – *adinnadana veramani* – not just to refrain from stealing, but to respect the property of others; not to disturb or misuse that which belongs to others. This is a way of making that very definite in our consciousness.

Abrahmacariya veramani, the third precept, is the vow of celibacy. This is a time when there's so much concern about AIDS and venereal diseases. A total misuse of sexuality has taken place over the past few decades whereby people have been totally irresponsible and sought pleasure from sexual activities without regard to the consequences. The result is that now we have moral dilemmas about abortion and the various diseases and problems which arise and how to solve them. What should we do? Try to promote the use of condoms and other prophylactic measures, so that people can do everything they want without having to restrain themselves? Or promote pills and devices to prevent pregnancy so that no-one will have to choose between having an abortion or having a baby? In all this debate, what is never even mentioned is any kind of moral position. It seems to be something you just don't mention. Celibacy is never even considered as a possible way of life.

---

*A lunar observance day,

42

But really, when we consider our life as human beings, there's a more skilful way to live. We can take responsibility for our existence and refrain from involving others or even exploiting our own bodies for the pursuit of that kind of pleasure. To undertake the precept of celibacy is rather ennobling. It lifts us up: to be celibate is a potential, a possibility for developing meditation through the restraint necessary for the realisation of truth. Celibacy is something one has to take on for oneself; it's not something which can be forced. That would not be chastity anymore; it would be tyranny. We must choose it and rise up to it as individual beings. We don't want to go back to a puritanical position of 'Thou shalt not', threatening people with 84,000 aeons in fiery hells burning in absolute pain for any kind of sexual enjoyment. We are not trying to bring fear into the mind or to intimidate, but rather to encourage what is noble and beautiful in our humanity.

I assume that you are capable of motivating yourself, and so I present this opportunity for practice. Sometimes people can have very low opinions of themselves which are not really true. Maybe they've never had an opportunity or never felt that anyone trusted them enough to motivate themselves. We are trying to bring into our monastic life that kind of value, that kind of beauty, so that monasticism is something that is 'beautiful in the beginning, beautiful in the middle and beautiful in the end', and not a kind of imposed tyranny or a forced march.

We need to take on that responsibility for ourselves rather than turning it over to somebody else, expecting someone else to and enlighten, love, drive or scold us. The spiritual potential of each being here is to be recognised. We have that marvellous ability to rise up to things rather than to sink down.

'Rising up' isn't a wilful force; it's the ability to go beyond the inertia or the habit tendencies of one's life toward something higher; it is learning how to just pay attention to the breath or to be more patient, more forgiving, more kindly – with oneself and others. All of this is the effort of rising up and meeting the occasion. This doesn't mean always having to succeed or prove oneself; it means rising up to meet a situation in a skilful way with mindfulness and wisdom. And this is a possibility for us: we don't have to be caught in the force of habit and lost in the realm of delusion.

With speech, *musavada veramani*, the precept is to refrain from incorrect speech: how easy it is to get caught in self-view if we use the 'I am' / 'poor me' speech habits! Notice the way the Buddha used

43

language: 'there is' suffering, 'there is' anger / greed / delusion. This is an example of refraining from wrong speech. If we start reflecting in that way, it affects how we see things. In this community, we have a willingness to learn how to communicate and we try to speak in a way which is clear and honest, but not demanding or deluding. By contrast, in society, one tries to be clever in one's speech, witty, droll – and, with an intelligent mind, one's speech habits can be quite cruel and unskilful. But we give that up and try to use speech as something beautiful and clear, without creating wrong veiws in the minds of others.

Musavada veramani is not just refraining from lies, but involves the intention to take on the responsibility for speaking. That whole function of our humanity is quite a miracle when you contemplate it. And yet we just take it for granted. We can use our speech for telling dirty jokes, cursing and swearing, gossiping, insulting and all kinds of mean, horrible and dishonest things; or we can respect this rather marvellous gift we have and learn how to use it in a way that is beautiful, accurate and kindly.

Then with *surameraya majjapamadatthana veramani* – refraining from intoxicants: think how fortunate we are that we don't have to drink, take drugs and shoot up heroin. That affects all levels of society. Men, women and children – all races, all classes are being caught in the grip of these addictive drugs. There are also cigarettes and alcohol – all harmful and deluding to the human mind. When we become clouded with drugs and drink, then we can't be responsible for what we say, can we?

I remember when I used to drink, it was so that I didn't have to be responsible for what I said! When intoxicated, you lose your sense of timidity and shame with regard to sexual conduct. You have a few drinks and suddenly, a lot of inhibitions just drop away. I wasn't into murdering people, but I certainly had no hesitation about getting rid of annoying insects and other things that I didn't like. One could see, under drugs and drink, how easily one's sense of moral propriety and commitment could disappear. Nowadays you find young people prostituting themselves to get money to buy drink and drugs – even people twelve or thirteen years old, those whom we used to call children!

Then there are the renunciant precepts, those which simplify our lives; to refrain from eating after noon and from entertainment and self-adornment. For human beings, there is a whole realm of fun and entertainment available through eating, dancing, singing, games, movies, TV and shows. Then there's sleep. There's the temptation to spend a great deal of time seeking comfort and sleep. Now these aren't immoral, are they? I'm not saying that eating a dinner is an immoral activity – or dancing and singing, come to that – but we are trying to restrain ourselves and refrain from opportunities to distract ourselves through sensory pleasures so that we can observe and reflect.

These are standards and precepts for reflection and not rules from God. They are not to be viewed from the 'Thou shalt not' position. Each one of the precepts is a resolution, something we are taking on and not something God is imposing on us. So you rise up to these precepts. You make a resolution in order to have it in your minds when you are tempted to act on the impulses you might be experiencing. After all, most of us come from backgrounds which were quite indulgent and where we were never really encouraged to restrain ourselves.

Sila is an honourable and lovely opportunity we have as human beings. We *choose* to be moral. We're not being moral because we're afraid of being immoral. We choose to do this and rise up to that which is noble, good, kind and generous.

Admittedly, worldly attractions remain strong and it isn't part of my teaching to condemn them. I'm not against the worldly life nor am I trying to raise monasticism up as something everyone should be doing. One can live a very good, wholesome worldly life too – wholesomeness is not just the prerogative of monks and nuns, is it? Sometimes lay people think I'm a 'monk fanatic' because I emphasise the value of this way of living.

But the attitude is one of reflection, rather than having an axe to grind or a position to adopt on things. We aim to develop that reflective ability of the mind – and the particular conventions we use are developed around that. This is what the Buddha's teaching is about. The whole convention of the Vinaya (discipline) and Dhamma teachings is to help in that way. Some people say you can do it as a lay person, and this is not to be denied; but if you can't use the lifestyle which is deliberately established for Dhamma-Vinaya, what makes you think you'll ever do it in any other form? This is what I want to get you to look at. Look at yourselves; at that wanting something you don't have or wanting to get away from what you have. Just watch that in yourself, that restlessness, discontentment and movement of your mind.

Sometimes, of course, one doesn't want to give up yet; one still wants rebirth and happiness and worldly things. Fair enough! But I don't want you to go round lying to yourselves. If you want to have your own way, have rebirths and worldly happiness. Then that's your decision – but don't delude yourselves by thinking that you are doing something else.

If you really understand the teaching of the Buddha, then there's nowhere to go and nothing to do. This is the way it is. We are living a life that is for that kind of reflection. Then you can observe that desire to be somewhere else as a movement of your mind, to see that and recognise it for what it is. Whether you do that or not is still up to you!

Allow yourself to die to the moment. Investigate and observe how things are. Everything that arises ceases. In all, everything fits into that pattern, doesn't it? In this way we can just reflect upon the day-to-day mundane ordinariness of our lives. Since we can't dance and sing, go to shows, pubs, football games, restaurants and follow the pleasures and distractions of the world, then the ordinariness of our lives takes on more significance. If you're used to a high level of excitement, ordinary things are just boring and one is always aiming at some new thrill or experience. Monasticism is a boring life-style, just a routine. We don't aim at distractions or having exciting things to do, because in meditation we are being aware of how things ordinarily are in consciousness.

So we're no longer trying to find and follow the extraordinary. It is only through calming down and restraint, not through following restlessness and being caught up in emotions that we have a chance to realise the Unconditioned. It's only when we can let go, calm down and reflect that there is a realisation of the ending of the conditioned realm – in which everything that arises ceases – and a realisation of Nibbana. There is no way of realising Nibbana by striving, trying to attain and achieve and being caught up in the arising aspect of life. You have to let go of that.

The realisation of letting go of what arises in the mind leads to witnessing the cessation of that which has arisen. Then there is the true peace of allowing things to be as they are and we are no longer acting like somebody who has to get somewhere, do something, get rid of something or change something. When we're caught in distracting ourselves with pleasures, then we're somebody who has to find happiness or have success or become something. No matter how much excitement and pleasures we might experience, we have to have more than that. We are never content with the excitement and adventures of life. They just cause us to be caught up in that movement of having to have more and more – until we get burnt out. Then we go to the opposite extreme – tired and worn out from all the excitement and stimulation, we just break down, fall asleep, get drugged or drunk. We do not want to exist. We can only have so much excitement and then we can't bear it any more.

To be excited continuously is a hell realm, isn't it? In my sister's home in California, they have all these television stations and cable relays. You can sit and have about seventy channels at your disposal all the time. People get into the habit of just switching channels if anything gets the slightest bit boring or slightly uninteresting or unpleasant. They just switch on to the next one – there's always a gun-fight or a chorus line to zap you. It's a kind of hell realm – it's unpleasant to have a mind that has to be stimulated one moment after another.

So you see the loveliness of a life that is based on composure, moral restraint, nobility, generosity, kindness and reflection upon Dhamma. It is wonderful to be able to have the opportunity and the encouragement to contemplate your own existence, and to train in a way that enables you to respect yourself. You can move toward being a contented and joyful person rather than a hungry and obsessed one.

'THE WAY IT IS'

A skilful reflection is: 'This is the way it is.' Venerable Buddhadasa Bhikkhu, the renowned Thai sage, said, 'If there was to be a useful inscription to put on a medallion around your neck, it would be "This is the way it is".' This reflection helps us to contemplate: wherever we happen to be, whatever time and place, good or bad, 'This is the way it is.' It is a way of bringing an acceptance into our minds, a noting rather than a reaction.

The practice of meditation is reflecting on 'the way it is' in order to see the fears and desires which we create. This is quite a simple practice, but the practice of Dhamma *should* be very very simple rather than complicated. Many methods of meditation are very complicated with many stages and techniques so one becomes addicted to complicated things. Sometimes because of our attachment to views, we don't really know how things are. However, the more simple we get, the more clear, profound and meaningful everything is to us.

For example, consider the people here, the monks and nuns we live with. Maybe some we feel attracted to, some we feel averse to, some we sympathise with, some we understand, some we don't understand; but whatever view we have, we can see it as just a 'view' of a person, rather than a real person. We can hear ourselves saying, 'I don't want him to be like that . . . I want him to be otherwise. He shouldn't be like this.'

'I want it to be otherwise' is the wail of the age, isn't it? Why can't life be otherwise? Why do people have to die? Why do we have to get old? Why this sickness? Why do we have to be separated from our loved ones? Why do innocent children who wouldn't hurt anyone in their lives, old people who wouldn't hurt anyone – why do they have to suffer from starvation or brutality?

There is always some new horrible thing happening. The other day someone wrote to me about the Bangladesh Muslims trying to get rid of Buddhist Hill Tribes in the Chittagong Hill Tracts through genocide. Then we hear about Iranians trying to eradicate the Bahais . . . it goes on endlessly. The Sinhalese and the Tamils. . . . There's always this clash between groups . . . one trying to take over another's land or power.

This has been going on since who knows when. There's always been someone trying to exterminate someone else since Cain murdered Abel – and that was a long time ago! But each time we hear of these atrocities we say 'How terrible . . . it shouldn't be. . . .'

We hear about American drug companies selling poisonous and horrible drugs to the Third World countries. 'That shouldn't be! Dreadful.' The pollution of the planet, the despoiling of the environment, the killing of dolphins and whales . . . where does it end? What can you do about it? It seems to be an endless problem of human ignorance. At a time when people should know better, they are doing the most horrendous things to each other. It is a time of gloomy predictions . . . earthquakes, volcanic eruptions and diseases . . . it shouldn't be like this.

Now saying, 'This is the way it is' is not an approval, or a refusal to do anything, but it is a way of establishing oneself in the knowledge that Nature is 'like this'. In the animal kingdom it's very much a question of survival of the fittest, a natural self-selecting law where the weaker strains are destroyed. So in that way even Nature is quite brutal, isn't it? We think of Nature as being everything it 'should' be . . . sweet, with flowers and sunshine – but Nature is also very brutal.

What is *our* position in Nature? We can live on the level of the animal kingdom where survival of the fittest is emphasised: the strong over the weak; living by fear and power. We can live like that because we share that animal mentality. We have an animal body and it has to survive like any other animal body on this planet. So the Law of the jungle is something human beings can subscribe to – which many of them do.

But this is only a lower level, isn't it? If we just live on that level then we must expect the world to be as it is – in a state of fear and anxiety. But as human beings we can get beyond this animal level; we can decide to abide by moral standards so that we don't have to live our lives in a state of anxiety.

But even higher than that is our ability to realise the Truth – to contemplate existence, to cultivate the reflective mind through which we can transcend personality. At the level of moral behaviour we still have a very strong personality view. And in our civilisation, we've developed a sense of 'me' and 'mine' to absurdity. So strong is this sense of 'me' and 'mine' that it seems to dominate and taint everything that we do, and there always a sense of anguish and suffering connected with it.

Just contemplate this: whenever there is a sense of 'me' and 'mine' in anything, it always seems to give rise to discontent or uncertainty, doubt, guilt, fear or anxiety. There is this view of 'me' as an individual being, of 'this' as mine, of what 'I' should or should not be or do, based on a belief in oneself as the body or a set of mental conditions.

However, this view is based on illusion; it comes from conditioning, not from insight. So as long as we identify with the limitations of the body and the mind then of course we are going to experience doubt, despair, anguish, sorrow, grief, and lamentation – these mental forms of suffering. How could it be otherwise? We're certainly not going to get enlightenment from distorted misunderstanding and wrong view.

We have this opportunity now to establish Right View and Right Understanding which frees us from the personality illusion: the identification with what are called the five aggregates – body, feeling, perception, mental formations and consciousness. So we contemplate the consciousness through the senses – eye, ear, nose, tongue and body. We can contemplate mental formations, the yesterdays of our own creation and the thoughts and views that we create. We can see them as impermanent.

We have the ability to contemplate the nature of things, to say, 'This is the way it is'. We can notice 'the way it is' without adapting a personality viewpoint. So with the breath of the body, the weight of its posture, we are just witnessing and noting how it is *now*, in *this* moment. The mood of the mind, whether we feel bright or dull, happy or unhappy, is something we can *know* – we can witness. And the empty mind, empty of the proliferations about oneself and others, is clear. It is intelligent and compassionate. The more we really look into the habits we have developed, the more clear things become for us. So we must be willing to suffer, to be bored, miserable and anguished: it's an opportunity to bear with these unpleasant mental states rather than suppress them. Having been born, *this* is the way it is at *this* time, at *this* place.

THE RAFT

The Buddha pointed to the way of seeing things as they are; this is what we mean by 'enlightenment'. Seeing the way it actually is, we aren't doomed to living in a realm which there's no way out of. There's a clear way out of that realm of misery; a very precise way. So the Buddha said, 'I teach only two things: suffering and the end of suffering.'

Buddhism is a baffling religion to Westerners because it has no doctrinal position. It makes no doctrinal statements about ultimate reality or anything: there's just suffering and the end of suffering. That is to be realised now; to realise the end of suffering you have to admit and really know what suffering is because the problem isn't with the suffering but with the delusion and the grasping. And we really have to *understand* suffering – according to the sermon of the Four Noble Truths, there is suffering and it should be understood.

In our daily life here at Amaravati, we notice when we are suffering. We can blame it on the weather, on the people or on something else, but that's not the point; because even if someone is treating us badly, that's just the way the world is. Sometimes people treat us well, sometimes they treat us badly because of this worldly concern for conditions; but the suffering is something we create.

In a monastery, we try to act in responsible ways so as not to intentionally cause anyone to suffer. We're here to encourage each other towards moral responsibility, co-operation, kindness and compassion. That's our intention.

Sometimes we get lost – we blow up at each other, or we do things that aren't very nice – but that's not our intention; these are the heedless moments. I conduct myself in a moral way not only for my own benefit, for my own practice, but out of respect for you and the Sangha, for the community around us: to be someone who lives within the restraints of the moral precepts.

Then my intention is towards my relationship with you, towards *metta*, kindness and compassion, joy, calm and serenity. At least the intention for everyone of us is to do good and refrain from doing evil. in a community with this kind of aspiration, we can really look at the suffering we create despite that. A lot of you really suffer here, and this is to be understood. It's the First Noble Truth, *dukkha*, the suffering of not getting what we want; the suffering of things not being the way we want them, of separation from what we like; the suffering of having to do that which we don't want to do, of having to be restrained when we want to be unrestrained.

I think of how easy it is to create you in my mind. 'The nuns are like this, the anagarikas are like that, bhikkhus are like this,' and so forth. One can have these biases: 'Women are this way, men are that way, Americans are like this and the English are like that.' We can believe that, but these are perceptions of the mind, views that arise and cease. And yet we can create a lot of suffering through them. 'This one doesn't come to the morning chanting or that one isn't doing their share of the work and this one thinks they're too important'; but the important point is the suffering, the *dukkha*, because when we have that, we create despair in our minds. We get annoyed and indignant and that all takes us to despair. If we don't understand *dukkha* here, then we're not going to understand it wherever we are: in London or in Bangkok or in Washington DC; on a mountain top or in a valley; with the good people or the bad people. So it's really important to observe suffering to know the *dukkha*.

There are three insights into the First Noble Truth: there is *dukkha*; it should be understood; it has been understood. That's how insight works; we recognise it; we understand it; and we begin to know when we understand it. So those are the three insights into the First Noble Truth.

The Second Noble Truth is the origin of *dukkha*: there is an origin; it's due to the grasping of desire. The second insight of the Second Noble Truth is that this attachment to desire – this identification with desire being 'me' and 'mine', this following of desire – should be let go of, leaving it as it is. Then the third insight of the Second Noble Truth is: desire has been let go of – through practice *dukkha* has been let go of.

There is the first insight into each of the truths: *pariyatti* – an observing that there *is* suffering, its origin, and so forth. Then there's the *patipatti* or the insight into practice; what we do; how we practise. And then the third insight is the *pativedha* or the wisdom. It has been understood; it has been let go of.

Now when there's that insight: 'The origin of suffering has been let go of', there is knowledge of that result – actually letting go. You know what it's like not to be attached to something. Like this clock. This is holding the clock; it's like this. And *now* I'm aware of what it's like not holding the clock. If I'm holding things and I'm heedless, then I don't even notice I'm not holding things. When there's no grasping, I'm not aware of it. A really ignorant and heedless person is so caught up with grasping that even though they're not grasping something all the time, the habit is such that they only notice when they are grasping at something. Now for example, many of you feel fully alive only when you're filled with greed or anger of some form or other. So letting go can be quite frightening to people; when they let go of things, they feel like they're no longer alive.

There's a lot of investment in being a person. Even the view that 'I have a bad temper; I have a lot of anger,' can be a kind of conceit. If I'm angry I feel very much alive. Sexual desire makes the 'I' feel alive – and that's why there's so much obsession with sex in modern European lives. And when there's no sexual desire, no anger, I want to fall asleep. I'm nothing. When there's no mindfulness at all, one just has to seek more sensual pleasure – to eat something, to drink something, take drugs or watch TV, read something or do something dangerous. You can break the law just because it's exciting to do so.

Now imagine trying to get people to spend a weekend just holding a clock noticing what it is like holding a clock! What a waste of time. I could be out terrorising the police; I could be at a disco – with strobe lights, music blaring in my ears, with pot and L.S.D. and Scotch! Being attentive to the way things are and no longer just distracting the mind sounds really painful by comparison.

This evening we're going to sit in meditation until midnight. It's a chance to observe more fully what it's like to be sitting; what it's like when the mind is filled with thoughts and when there are no thoughts; when there is suffering and when there is no suffering. If you have a view that sitting until midnight is going to be suffering, you have already committed yourself to suffering until midnight.

But if you start examining that very view or fear or doubt in your mind for what it is, you can observe when it's present and when it's not present. If you're suffering, then you're not thinking there's any suffering. You have this feeling of suffering and you're attached to the view 'I'm suffering and I have to sit up and I'm tired.' So the First Noble Truth: 'there's suffering; suffering is to be understood', is actually experienced through an admission, a recognition and an understanding.

The insight of the Second Noble Truth is to let go of it, to leave it alone – don't make anything out of an all-night sitting. These are perceptions. They're nothing, really: if you're using the situation for reflection and contemplation of when there is suffering – then there isn't any suffering. I'm aware of holding this thought, grasping this thought or of not grasping this thought. One can pick things up or put them down, knowing how to use these things rather than having a blind obsession to grasp or reject. I can put down the clock, but I don't have to throw it away, do I? It's not that holding the clock is wrong unless there is ignorance about it. One is aware of the grasping and the non-grasping, holding and not holding.

The Third Noble Truth is that there is the cessation of suffering. When you let go of something and you realise letting go, your habits become your teachers. When you let go of suffering, suffering ceases. 'There is cessation and it should be realised' – this is the second insight into the Third Noble Truth. And this is our practice: to realise cessation, to notice when suffering ceases. It's not that everything's going to disappear, but the feeling of suffering and 'I am' ceases. This is not to be believed, but to be realised – and then there is the third insight: that cessation has been realised.

This leads to the insight into the Fourth Noble Truth concerning the Eightfold Path, the Way out of suffering. These insights connect to one another. It's not that first you do one and then you do the other – they support each other. As we have the insight into letting go, as we realise cessation, then there is Right Understanding and the rest follows from that – the development of wisdom or *pañña*.

Now don't see this as something that deals only with very deep and important issues, because it's about the here and now, the way things are. We're not just working with extreme situations, but just with sitting, standing, walking, lying down, breathing, feeling as normal beings and living in a moral environment with the way it is. We don't have to go into Hell to really see suffering; we're not seeking it out.

We can create Hell at Amaravati, not because Amaravati is Hell, but because we create it with all kinds of miserable things from our mind; and this is the suffering we can work with. This is the suffering of the normal human realm where our intentions are to refrain from doing evil, to do good, to develop virtue and to be kind. There's still enough suffering here to contemplate these Four Noble Truths in their twelve aspects.

You can memorise them; then, wherever you are, you've got something to contemplate. Eventually, you let go of all these things because they're not ends in themselves either, but they are like tools to be used. You learn to use these tools, and when you've finished you don't need to hang on to them.

Signifying this, the Buddha referred to his teaching as a raft which you can make out of the things around you. You don't have to have a special motor boat or submarine or luxury liner. A raft is something you make from the things around just to cross to the other shore. We're not trying to make a super-duper vehicle; we can use what's around us for enlightenment. The raft is to carry us across the sea of ignorance and when we get to the other shore, we can let it go – which doesn't mean you have to throw it away.

This 'other shore' can also be a delusion, because 'the other shore' and this shore are really the same. It's merely an allegory. We have never really left the other shore, we've always been on the other shore anyway; and the raft is something we use to remind us that we don't really need a raft. So there's absolutely nothing to do, except to be mindful, to sit, stand, walk, lie down, eat your food, breathe – all the opportunities as humans to do good. We have this lovely opportunity in the human realm to be good, to be kind, to be generous, to love others, to serve and help others. This is one of the loveliest qualities of being human.

We can decide not to do evil. We don't have to kill, lie, steal, distract ourselves and drug ourselves or get lost in moods and feelings. We can be free from all that. It's a wonderful opportunity in the human form to refrain from evil and to do good – not in order to store up merit for the next life, but because this is the beauty of our humanity. Being a human can be a joyful experience rather than an onerous task.

And so, when we contemplate this, we begin to really appreciate this birth in a human form. We feel grateful to have this opportunity to live with our teacher, the Buddha, and our practice, the Dhamma; and to live in the Sangha.

Sangha represents the human community as unified in virtuousness and moral restraint; it is the soul force of the human realm. That which is truly benevolent in humanity has its effect on the moral forces that abide in the human realm. So all sentient beings are benefited by that. What would it be like if there were just a selfish humanity with every man for himself, endlessly making demands, not caring about each other at all? It would be a terrible place to live. Therefore we don't do that; we abide in the Sangha, an abiding where we live together within a convention that encourages morality and respect for each other. This is for reflection, for contemplation; you have to know it for yourself; nobody can realise it for you. You have to arouse yourself, and not depend on something external to push you or support you.

We even have to let go of our need to be inspired. We have to develop the strength to where we no longer need any kind of inspiration or encouragement from anyone else – because inspiration isn't wisdom, is it? You get high – 'Ajahn Sumedho's wonderful' – and then after a while you don't get high on me any more, and then: 'Ajahn Sumedho's disappointing; he's let me down.' Inspiration is like eating chocolate: it tastes good and it's very attractive but it's not going to nourish you; it only energises you momentarily and that's all it can do. So it's not wise to depend on other people living in the way that you want them to and never disappointing you.

It's so important to develop insight through practice, because inspiration just wears out – and if you are attached and blinded by it, then you are in for terrible disillusionment and bitterness. There's so much of this with different charismatic, guru-figures that teach around the world. It's not balanced, is it? As intoxicated as you can get with somebody else's charisma, you can't maintain it. So it inevitably involves falling down into some lower state.

The way of mindfulness is, however, always appropriate to the time and the place, to the way things are in their good and bad aspects. Then suffering isn't dependent on the world being good or bad, but on how willing we are to use wisdom in this present moment. The way out of suffering is *now*, in being able to see things as they are.

PATIENCE

Peacefulness and tranquillity can be incredibly boring, and can bring up a lot of restlessness and doubt. Restlessness is a common problem because the sensory realm is a restless realm; bodies are restless and minds are restless. Conditions are changing all the time, so if you are caught up in reacting to change, you're just restless.

Restlessness needs to be thoroughly understood for what it is; the practice is not one of just using the will to bind yourself to the meditation mat. It's not a test of you becoming a strong person who has to conquer restlessness – that attitude just reinforces another egotistical view. But it is a matter of really investigating restlessness, noticing it and knowing it for what it is. For this we have to develop patience; it's something we have to learn and really work with.

When I first went to Wat Pah Pong, I couldn't understand Lao. And in those days Ajahn Chah was at his peak and giving three-hour *desanas* every evening. He could go on and on and on, and everybody loved him – he was a very good speaker, very humorous and everybody enjoyed his talks. But if you couldn't understand Lao . . .!

I'd be sitting there thinking, 'When's he going to stop, I'm wasting my time.' I'd be really angry, thinking, 'I've had enough, I'm leaving.' But I couldn't get enough nerve to leave, so I would just sit there thinking – 'I'll go to another monastery. I've had enough of this; I'm not going to put up with this.' And then he would look at me – he had the most radiant smile – and he'd say, 'Are you all right?' And suddenly all the anger that had been accumulating for that three hours would completely drop away.

That's interesting, isn't it? After sitting there fuming for three hours, it can just go. So I vowed that my practice would be patience, and that during this time I would develop patience. I'd come to all the talks and sit through all of them as long as I could physically stand it. I determined not to miss them, or try to get out of them, and just practise patience.

And by doing that I began to find that the opportunity to be patient was something that has helped me very much. Patience is a very firm foundation for my insight and understanding of the Dhamma; without that I would have just wandered and drifted about, as you see so many people doing. Many Westerners came to Wat Pah Pong and drifted away from it because they weren't patient. They didn't want to sit through three-hour *desanas* and be patient. They wanted to go to the places where they could get instant enlightenment and get it done quickly in the way that they wanted.

Through the selfish desires and ambitions which can drive us, even on the spiritual path, we can't really appreciate the way things are. When I reflected and actually contemplated my life at Wat Pah Pong, I realised that it was a very good situation: there was a good teacher, there was enough to eat, the monks were good monks, the lay people were very generous and kind and there was encouragement towards the practice of Dhamma. This is as good as you can get; it was a wonderful opportunity. And yet so many Westerners couldn't see that because they tended to think – 'I don't like this, I don't want that; it should be otherwise.' And – 'What *I* think is . . . what *I* feel is. . . I don't want to be bothered with *this* and *that*.'

I remember going up to Tam Sang Phet monastery, which was a very quiet secluded place in those years, and I lived in a cave. A villager built me a platform because in the bottom of this cave was a big python. One evening I was sitting on this platform by candlelight. It was really eerie and the light cast shadows on all the rocks: it was weird, and I started to get really frightened and then, suddenly, I was startled. I looked up and there was a huge owl right above, looking at me. It looked immense – I don't know if it was that big, but it seemed really enormous in the candlelight – and it was looking straight at me. I thought, 'Well what is there to be really frightened of here?' and I tried to imagine skeletons and ghosts or Mother Kali with fangs and blood dripping out of her mouth or enormous monsters with green skin – than I began to laugh because it got so amusing! I realised I wasn't really frightened at all.

In those days, I was just a very junior monk and one night Ajahn Chah took me to a village fête – I think Satimanto Bhikkhu was there at the time. We were *very* serious practitioners, and we didn't want any kind of frivolity or foolishness. And of course going to a village fête was the *last thing* we wanted to do – because in these villages they love loudspeakers. Anyway, Ajahn Chah took Satimanto and me to this fête, and we had to sit up all night with the raucous sounds of the loudspeakers – and monks giving talks all night long! I kept thinking, 'Oh, I want to get back to my cave – green-skinned monsters and ghosts are much better than this.' I noticed that Satimanto, who was *incredibly* serious, was looking really angry and critical and very unhappy. We just sat there looking miserable. I thought, 'Why does Ajahn Chah bring us to these things?'

Then I began to see for myself. I remember sitting there thinking, 'Here I am getting all upset over this. Is it that bad? What's really bad is what I'm making out of it. What's really miserable is my mind. Loudspeakers and noise, and distraction and sleepiness, I can put up with, but it's that awful thing in my mind that hates it, resents it and wants to leave – that's the real misery!'

That evening I saw what misery I could create in my mind over things that actually I could bear. I remember that as a very clear insight into what I *thought* was miserable, and what *really is* miserable. At first I was blaming the people, the loudspeakers, the disruption, the noise and the discomfort – I thought that was the problem. Then I realised that it wasn't; it was my mind that was miserable.

If we reflect on and contemplate Dhamma, we learn from the very situations which we like the least – if we have the will and the patience to do so.

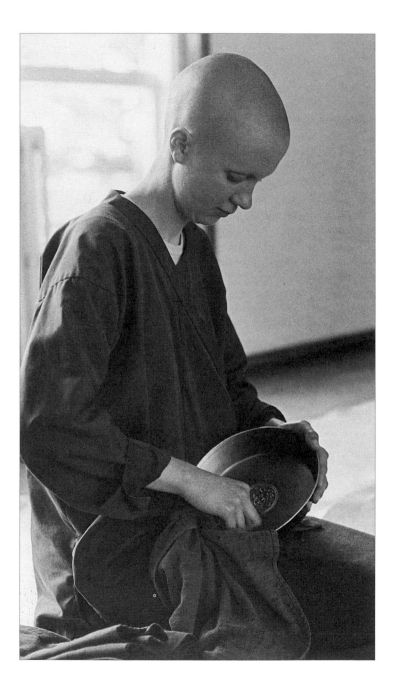

reflections on food

Wisely reflecting on this alms-food
I use it not to distract my mind
Nor to gratify desire,
Not to make my form impressive
Or to make it beautiful,
Simply to be sustained and nourished
And to maintain what health I have
To help fulfill the Holy Life;
　　With this attitude in mind,
'I will allay hunger without overeating
So that I may continue to live blamelessly and at ease.'

ACCEPTING THE WAY
THINGS ARE

How many of you have been practising today trying to become something 'I have got to do this . . . or become that . . . or get rid of something . . . or got to do something. . . .' That compulsiveness takes over, even in our practice of Dhamma. 'This is the way it is' isn't a fatalistic attitude of not caring or being indifferent, but is a real openness to the way things have to be at this moment. For example, right now at this moment this is the way it is and it can't be any other way at this moment. It's so obvious, isn't it?

Right now, no matter whether you are feeling high or low or indifferent, happy or depressed, enlightened or totally deluded, half-enlightened, half-deluded, three-quarters deluded, one-quarter enlightened, hopeful or despairing – this is the way it is. And it can't be any other way at this moment.

How does your body feel? Just notice that the body is *this* way. It's heavy, it's earthbound, it's coarse, it gets hungry, it feels heat and cold, it gets sick, sometimes it feels very nice, sometimes it feels very horrible. This is the way it is. Human bodies are like this; so that this tendency to want it to be otherwise falls away. It doesn't mean we can't try to make things better, but we do so from understanding and wisdom rather than from an ignorant desire.

The world is this way and things happen, and it snows and the sun comes out, and people come and go, people have misunderstandings, people's feelings get hurt. People get lazy, and inspired and people get depressed and disillusioned, people gossip and disappoint each other and there is adultery and there's theft, drunkenness and drug addiction and there are wars, and there always have been.

Here in a community like Amaravati we can see the way things are. Now it's the weekend and more people come to offer alms-food and it's more crowded and noisy and sometimes there are children

64

running up and down screaming and people pounding vegetables and chopping things and everything going all over the place. You can observe 'This is the way it is' rather than 'These people are impinging on my silence.' 'I don't want it to be like that, I want it to be otherwise,' might be the reaction if you like the quiet orderliness of the meal where there's none of that going on and there are no loud noises or harsh sounds. But life is like this, this is the way life is, this is human existence. So in our minds we embrace the whole of it, and 'This is the way it is' allows us to accept the changes and movements from the silent to the noisy, from the controlled and ordered to the confused and muddled.

One can be a very selfish Buddhist and want life to be very quiet and want to be able to 'practise' and have plenty of time for sitting, plenty of time for studying the Dhamma and 'I don't want to have to receive guests and talk to people about silly things' and 'I don't want to . . . blah blah blah.' You can really be a very, very selfish person as a Buddhist monk. You can want the world to align itself with your dreams and ideals and, when it doesn't, you don't want it anymore. But rather than make things the way you want them, the Buddha way is to notice the way things are. And it's a great relief when you accept the way it is, even if it's not very nice; because the only real misery is not wanting it to be like that.

Whether things are going not so well or well, if we're not accepting the way things are, then the mind tends to be creating some form of misery. So, if you are attached to things going nicely, then you'll start worrying about them if they don't go so well, even when things are actually going well. I have just noticed that with little things, such as when it's a sunny day and one jumps for joy – then the next thought will be, 'But in England you know, the sun can disappear in the next moment.'

As soon as I've grasped one perception and I'm jumping for joy at the sunshine, then the unpleasant thought arises that it may not last. Whatever you're attached to will bring on its opposite. And then when things aren't going very well, the mind tends to think, 'I want them to get better than this.' So suffering arises wherever there is this grasping of desire.

The sensory world is pleasurable and painful, it's beautiful and ugly, it's neutral; there are all gradations, all possibilities in it. This is just what sensory experience is about. But when there's ignorance and the self-view operating, I only want pleasure and I don't want pain. I want only beauty and I don't want ugliness. 'Please God, please make me healthy, give me a good complexion, physical attractiveness, and let me stay young for a long time, get lots of money, wealth and power, no sickness, no cancer, lots of beautiful things around me, surround me with beauty and the pleasures of the senses at their best, please.' Then the fear will come that maybe I'll get the worst. I could get leprosy, AIDS, Parkinson's disease or cancer. And I might be rejected and despised and humiliated and left alone out in the cold hungry, sick and in danger, with the wolves howling and the wind blowing.

From the view-point of the self, there's a tremendous fear of rejection, ostracism or of being despised in our society. There's a fear of being left alone and unwanted, there's a fear of being old, and left to die alone, there's natural fear of physical danger, of being in situations where our bodies are in danger; and there's the fear of the unknown, the mysterious, the ghosts and the unseen spirits.

So we gravitate to security don't we? Cosy little places with electricity, central heating, insurance and guarantees on everything – rates paid and legal contracts. All of these give us a sense of safety or we seek emotional security. 'Say you'll always love me dear. Say you'll love me even if you don't mean it. Make everything safe and secure.' And in that demand there's always going to be anxiety because of the grasping at desire.

So we're developing a light around the uplifting of the human spirit rather than the material guarantees. As alms-mendicants, you're taking the risk that you might not get anything to eat. You might not have a shelter, you might not have any really good medicine, you might not have anything nice to wear. People are very generous, but as mendicants we don't take it for granted, assuming that we deserve it. We are grateful for whatever is offered, and cultivate the attitude of wanting and needing little. We need to make ourselves ready to leave and relinquish everything at any moment, to have the kind of mind that doesn't think, 'This is my home, I want it to be guaranteed for the rest of my life.'

No matter which way it goes, we adapt, to life, to time and place, rather than make demands. Whatever way it goes, is the way it is.

Whatever diseases I may get, or tragedies or catastrophes or successes or the best to the worst, one can say this is the way it is. And in that there is acceptance and non-anger, non-greed and the ability to cope with life as it's happening.

We are not here to become anything or to get rid of anything, to change anything or to make anything for ourselves, or to demand anything, but to awaken more and more, to reflect, observe and know the Dhamma. Don't worry that it might change for the worse. Whatever way it changes, we have the wisdom to adapt to it. And that I can see is the real fearlessness of the alms-mendicant life. We can adapt, we can wisely learn from all conditions, because this life-span is not our real home.

This life-span is a transition we're involved in, this is a journey through the sensory realm and there are no nests, no homes, no abiding in this sensory realm. It's all very impermanent, subject to disruption and change at any moment. That is its nature. That's the way it is. There is nothing depressing about that if you no longer make the demand for security in it.

The reality of existence is that there isn't any home here. So the homeless life, the going forth into mendicancy is what they call a heavenly messenger, because the religious spirit is no longer sharing the delusions of the worldly mind, which is very determined to have a material home and security. You have the trust in Buddha, Dhamma, Sangha and the teaching and the opportunities as mendicants and meditators for the insight and understanding to free the mind from the anxieties that come from the attachment to the sensory realm as a home.

The idea of owning and hanging on to things is the illusion of the worldly life. The view of the self sends forth all these delusions in which we have to protect ourselves all the time. We're always endangered, there's always something to be worried about, something to be frightened of. But when that illusion is punctured with wisdom, then there is fearlessness; we see this is a journey, a transition from the sensory realm and we are willing to learn the lessons it teaches us, no matter what those lessons might be.

CONSCIOUSNESS AND SENSITIVITY

Sometimes we approach meditation too much from an ideal of trying to control the mind and get rid of unwanted mental states. It can become an obsession. Meditation can be just another thing we have to *do*; this worldly attitude tends to affect whatever we're doing.

See meditation not as something for measuring yourself as a person, but as an occasion or opportunity to be mindful and be at peace with yourself and with whatever mood or state you happen to be in at this moment. Learn to be at peace with the way you are, rather than trying to become something, or achieve a state that you'd like to have.

That whole way of thinking is based on delusion. I remember when I started meditation in Thailand, all my ambitious and aggressive tendencies would start taking over. The way I'd lived my life would affect how I would approach meditation. So I began to notice that. I began to let go of things and to accept even those tendencies, and be attentive to the way it is. The more you trust in that, then the more quickly you will understand the Dhamma, the way out of suffering.

Notice how things affect your mind. If you've just come from your work or from your home, notice what it does to your mind. Don't criticise it – we're not here to blame or to think that there's something wrong with our profession if our mind isn't tranquil and pure and serene when we come here. But notice the business of life: having to talk to people, having to answer telephones, having to type or to travel across London in the rush hour. Maybe we're having to work with people that we don't like, in difficult, aggravating situations. Just notice – not to criticise, but just to accept, that these things do have an affect on us.

Recognise that this is the experience of consciousness and sensitivity. That's what being born as a human being amounts to, isn't it? You're born and you have to live a lifetime as a conscious being in a very sensitive form. So what impinges on you, what comes to you from the objective world, is going to affect you. It's just the way it is. There's nothing wrong with it. But then the ignorant human being takes it all personally, so we tend to make everything very personal. It's as if I *shouldn't* be affected by these things that impinge on me. I shouldn't feel anger or aversion or greed, or irritation and frustration, envy, jealousy, fear, anxiety. I shouldn't be feeling these things. If I were a normal, healthy man I wouldn't have any of these problems. If I were a normal, healthy man I wouldn't be sensitive at all! Like a rhinoceros – with a tough hide that nothing could ever get through.

But recognise that being human, we have these extremely sensitive forms. There's nothing really wrong with you. It's just the way it is. Life is like this. We live in a society that is just the way it is. Living in London or in suburbia – or anywhere – we can spend our time grumbling because it's not perfect. There are many things that are irritating in our lives. But then being sensitive is like this, isn't it? Sensitivity means that, whatever it is, whether it's pleasant or unpleasant, pleasurable, painful, beautiful, ugly – we're going to feel it.

And so the only way out of suffering is through mindfulness. When you're truly mindful there's no self. You're not taking life's experiences from the assumption of being a person. You can try to make yourself insensitive, say you close your eyes, put ear plugs in your ears and try to be totally insensitive, shut everything out – and that's one type of meditation, sensory deprivation. And if you stay that way for a while,then you feel very calm because nothing is demanded of you at that time. There's no kind of harsh or stimulating, exciting or frustrating impingement.

So, if you're mindful, you have an awareness of the purity of your mind which is blissful. Your true nature, then, is blissful and serene and pure. But then, if you still have the wrong view about it, you think, 'I have to have a sensory deprivation experience all the time. I can't live in London any more. Even the Buddhist Society* is too noisy!'

---

* The venue of this talk was in the meditation hall of the Buddhist
Society in Victoria, Central London.

If our peace and serenity depends upon conditions being a certain way, then we get very attached. We become enslaved, we want to control situations and then we become even more upset if anything disrupts them and gets in the way of our peace. 'I've got to find some place – a cave. I've got to get my own sensory deprivation tank and find the ideal situation. Set up all the conditions where I can keep everything at bay so I can just abide in the blissful serenity of the purity of the mind.' But then you see, that view is based on desire, isn't it? It's a self-view, a desire to have that experience because you remember it, liked it and want it again.

One time on a retreat, I heard some person who was having trouble swallowing. I was sitting there and that person would go 'gulp, gulp.' They weren't very loud but when you're attached to total silence, even a gulp can upset you. So I got quite irritated and wanted to throw that person out of the meditation hall. Reflecting on it, I realised that the fault was in me, not in the person.

But mindfulness and understanding the Dhamma allow you to adapt and accept life – the total life experience – without having to control it. With mindfulness, you don't have to hold on to bits and pieces that you like and then feel very threatened by the possibilities of being separated from them. Right meditation allows you to be very brave and adaptable, flexible with your life and all that that implies.

We don't have all that much control, do we? Much as we would like to be able to control our lives, we recognise we really don't have that much control. Some things just get out of our control. Things happen and Mother Nature has her ways of letting us know that She's not just going to follow our desires. Then fashions and revolutions, and changing conditions, and population problems, and airplanes, televisions, technology, pollution – how can we control it and make it so that we are not being affected by any of it, or only affected in the ways we like ?

If we spend our lives trying to control everything, then we just increase the suffering. Even if we should get a measure of control over things, get what we want, we're still going to be like me with the person gulping in the meditation hall; getting very angry when the neighbour turns on the radio too loud or the airplane flies low or the fire engine goes by.

Now one thing to recognise: when you have a body you have to live with it for a lifetime. And these bodies are conscious and sensitive forms. This is just the way it is, what being born means.

Bodies: they grow up, then they start getting old. And then there's old age, and then sicknesses, disease – this is a part of our human experience. And then death. We have to accept the death and separation of loved ones. This happens to all of us. Most of us will see our parents die, or even our children, or spouse or friends, loved ones. Part of all human experience is the experience of being separated from the loved.

By knowing the way it is, then you find yourself quite capable of accepting life and not being depressed and bewildered by the way life happens to be. Once you understand it and you see it in the right way, then you're not going to create any wrong views about it. You're not going to add to it with fears, and desires, and bitterness, and resentments and blame. We have the ability to accept the way life happens to us as individual beings. Even though we're terribly sensitive, we're also tough survivors in this universe.

You look at where human beings manage to live, like Eskimos up in the Arctic and people in deserts. In the most uninviting places on this planet, there's usually human habitation; when forced to we can survive anywhere.

Understanding Dhamma allows us also to have a fearless atti-tude. We begin to realise that we can accept whatever happens. There's really nothing to be afraid of. Then you can let go of life, you can follow it because you're not expecting anything out of it, and you're not trying to control it. You have the wisdom, the mindfulness, the ability to roll with the flow rather than to be drowned by the tidal waves of life.

Learn to take the time to be silent and listen to yourself. Use the breathing and the body, its natural rhythm, and the way your body *feels* now. Put your attention onto the body, because the body is a condition in Nature. It's not really you. It's not 'my' breathing any more, it's not personal; you breathe even if you're crazy, or sick – and if you're asleep you're still breathing. The body breathes. From birth to death it will be breathing. So breath is something that we use as an object to focus on, to turn to. If we think too much, our thoughts get very convoluted and complicated; but if we bring attention just to the ordinary breathing of the body at this moment, at that moment we're actually not thinking – we're attentive to a natural rhythm.

Then you might start making problems out of it: 'Oh, I can't concentrate on my breath, blah, blah, blah. . . .' Then it becomes 'me' again trying to be mindful of my breath. But actually in any one moment where you're just with the breath, there's no self. Your self will arise when you start thinking. When you're not thinking there's no self and when you're mindful, then the thought isn't coming from the wrong view that: 'I am a self'. Thought then can be a way of reflection, a way of focusing attention on Dhamma rather than creating problems, criticism, and anxiety, about myself and humanity.

Just contemplate: when you get angry you have to think, don't you? If you stop thinking, the anger will go away. To be angry you have to think: 'He said that to me, how dare he. That dirty so-and-so!' But if you should stop thinking and use the breath, eventually that feeling of the body that comes with anger will fade out and then there is no anger. So if you feel angry, just reflect on what it feels like as a physical feeling. It's the same with any mood: contemplate, reflect on the mood that you're in. Work with it – not to analyse it or criticise it, but merely to reflect on it how it is.

Sometimes people say: 'I get very confused when I meditate. How can I get rid of confusion?' Wanting to get rid of confusion is the problem. Being confused and not wanting it creates even *more* confusion.

So what does confusion feel like? Some of the more stimulating passions that we can have are quite obvious. What we tend to not pay any attention to, or dismiss, are the more subtle states like slight confusion, or hesitation, or doubt, insecurity and anxiety. And, of course, one side of us just wants to get rid of it, just stamp it out. How do I get rid of it? If I meditate, how can I get rid of my fears and anxiety?

With the right understanding, we see that the very desire 'to get rid of' is suffering. We can bear with the feeling of insecurity if we know what it is, and that it changes, it's impermanent. So more and more you begin to feel confident in just being aware and mindful rather than trying to develop your practice in order to become an enlightened person. The assumption is that right now you're not enlightened, you've got a lot of problems, you've got to change your life, you're got to make yourself different. You're not good enough the way you are right now, so you have to meditate and hopefully some time in the future, you'll become something that you'd like to become.

If you never see the delusion of that way of thinking, then it just carries on. You never really become what you should be. No matter how much effort you put into your meditations, after years of trying to become enlightened, you always feel like a failure because you've still got the wrong attitude about it all.

THE SOUND OF SILENCE

As you calm down, you can experience the sound of silence in the mind. You hear it as a kind of high frequency sound, a ringing sound that's always there. It is just normally never noticed. Now when you begin to hear that sound of silence, it's a sign of emptiness – of silence of the mind. It's something you can always turn to. As you concentrate on it and turn to it, it can make you quite peaceful and blissful. Meditating on that, you have a way of letting the conditions of the mind cease without supressing them with another condition. Otherwise you just end up putting one condition over another.

This process of putting one condition on top of another is what is meant by making 'kamma'. For example, if you're feeling angry, then you start thinking of something else to get away from the anger. You don't like what is going on over here, so you look over there, you just run away. But if you have a way of turning from conditioned phenomena to the unconditioned, then there is no kind of kamma being made, and the conditioned habits can fade away and cease. It's like a 'safety hatch' in the mind, the way out, so your kammic formations, sankharas, have an exit, a way of flowing away instead of re-creating themselves.

One problem with meditation is that many people find it boring. People get bored with emptiness. They want to fill up emptiness with something. So recognise that even when the mind is quite empty, the desires and habits are still there, and they will come and want to do something interesting. You have to be patient, willing to turn away from boredom and from the desire to do something interesting and be content with the emptiness of the sound of silence. And you have to be quite determined in turning towards it.

But when you begin to listen and understand the mind better, it's a very realisable possibility for all of us. After many years of practice, gross kammic formations fade away, while the more subtle ones also start to fade away. The mind becomes increasingly more empty and clear. But it takes a lot of patience, endurance and willingness to keep practising under all conditions, and to let go even of one's most treasured little habits.

One can believe that the sound of silence *is* something, or that it is an attainment. Yet it is not a matter of having attained anything, but of wisely reflecting on what you experience. The way to reflect is that anything that comes goes; and the practice is one of knowing things as they are.

I'm not giving you any kind of identity – there is nothing to attach to. Some people want to know, when they hear that sound, 'Is that stream entry?' or 'Do we have a soul?' We are so attached to the concepts. All we can know is that we want to know something, we want to have a label for our 'self'. If there is a doubt about something, doubt arises and then there is desire for something. But the practice is one of letting go. We keep with what is, recognising conditions as conditions and the unconditioned as the unconditioned. It's as simple as that.

Even religious aspiration is seen as a condition! It doesn't mean that you shouldn't aspire, but it just means that you should recognise aspiration in itself as being limited. And emptiness is not self either – attachment to the idea of emptiness is *also* attachment. *That* also is to be let go of! The practice then becomes one of turning away from conditioned phenomena, not creating anything more around the existing conditions. So whatever arises in your consciousness – anger or greed or anything – you recognise it is there but you make nothing out of it. You can turn to the emptiness of the mind – to the sound of silence. This gives the conditions like anger a way out to cessation; you let it go away.

We have memories of what we have done in the past, don't we? They come up in consciousness when the conditions are there for them to come. That is the resultant *kamma* of having done something in the past, having acted out of ignorance and having done things out of greed, hatred and delusion, and so forth. . . . When that *kamma* ripens in the present, one still has the impulses of greed, hatred and delusion that come up in the mind as the resultant *kamma*. Whenever we act on these ignorantly, when we aren't mindful, then we create more *kamma*.

The two ways we can create *kamma* are with following it or trying to get rid of it. When we stop doing these, the cycles of *kamma* have an opportunity to cease. The resultant *kamma* that has arisen has a way out, an 'escape hatch' to cessation.

ONLY ONE BREATH

This morning I was talking to Venerable Subbato and he was saying he never has developed *anapanasati*, mindfulness of the breath. So I said, 'Can you be mindful of one inhalation?' And he said, 'Oh yes.' 'And of one exhalation?' And he said, 'Yes.' And I said, 'Got it!'

There's nothing more to it than that. However, one tends to expect to develop some special kind of ability to go into some special state. And because we don't do that, then we think we can't do it.

But the way of the spiritual life is through renunciation, relinquishment, letting go *not through attaining or acquiring*. Even the jhanas* are relinquishments rather than attainments. If we relinquish more and more, letting go more and more, then the jhanic states are natural.

The attitude is most important. To practise *anapanasati*, one brings the attention onto one inhalation, being mindful from the beginning to the end. One inhalation, that's it; and then the same goes for the exhalation. That's the perfect attainment of *anapanasati*. The awareness of just that much is the result of concentration of the mind through sustained attention on the breath – from the beginning to the end of the inhalation, from the beginning to the end of the exhalation. The attitude is always one of letting go, not attaching to any ideas or feelings that arise from that, so that you're always fresh with the next inhalation, the next exhalation, completely as it is. You're not carrying over anything. So it's a way of relinquishment, of letting go, rather than of attaining and achieving.

The dangers in meditation practice is the habit of grasping at things, grasping at states; so the concept that's most useful is the concept of letting go, rather than of attaining and achieving. If you

---

jhanas: these are refined states of mind-consciousness experienced through meditative absorption.

say today that yesterday you had a really super meditation, absolutely fantastic, just what you've always dreamed of, and then today you try to get the same wonderful experience as yesterday, but you get more restless and more agitated than ever before – now why is that? Why can't we get what we want? It's because we're trying to attain something that we remember rather than really working with the way things are, as they happen to be now. So the correct way is one of mindfulness, of looking at the way it is now rather than remembering yesterday and trying to get to that state again.

The first year I meditated I didn't have a teacher. I was in this little *kuti** in Nong Khai for about ten months, and I had all kinds of blazing insights. Being alone for ten months, not having to talk, not having to go anywhere, everything calmed down after several months, and then I thought I was a fully enlightened person, an arahant. I was sure of it. I found out later that I wasn't.

I remember we went through a famine in Nong Khai that year and we didn't get very much to eat. I had malnutrition, so I thought, 'Maybe malnutrition's the answer. If I just starve myself. . . .' I remember being so weak with malnutrition at Nong Khai that my earlobes started cracking open. On waking up, I'd have to pry my eyelids open; they'd be stuck shut with the stuff that comes out of your eyelids when you're not feeling very well.

Then one day this Canadian monk brought me three cans of tinned milk. In Asia they have tinned sweetened milk and it's very very delicious. And he also brought me some instant coffee, and a flask of hot water. So I made a cup of this: put in a bit of coffee, poured in some of this milk, poured hot water and started drinking it. And I just went crazy. It was so utterly delicious, the first time I had anything sweet in weeks, or anything stimulating. And being malnourished and being in a very dull tired apathetic state, this was like high-octane petrol – whoomph! Immediately I gulped that down – I couldn't stop myself – and I managed to consume all three tins of milk and a good portion of that coffee. And my mind actually went flying into outer space, or it seemed like it, and I thought, 'Maybe that's the secret. If I can just get somebody to buy me tinned milk.'

When I went to Wat Pah Pong the following year I kept thinking, 'Oh, I had all those wonderful experiences in Nong Khai.

---

*kuti – a very simple unfurnished wooden hut that serves as a dwelling for a Buddhist monk or nun

I had all those beautiful visions, and all those fantastic floating experiences and blazing insights, and it seemed like I understood everything. And you even thought you were an arahant.' At Wat Pah Pong, that first year there, I didn't have much of anything. I just kept trying to do all the things I'd done in Nong Khai to get these things. But after a while, even using strong cups of coffee didn't work any more. I didn't seem to get those exhilarations, those fantastic highs and blazing insights, that I had the first year. So after the first *Vassa** at Wat Pah Pong, I thought, 'This place is not for me. I think I'll go and try to do repeat what happened in Nong Khai.' And I left Ajahn Chah and went to live on Pupek mountain in Sakorn Nakorn province.

There, at last, I was in an idyllic spot. However, for the alms-round there you had to leave before dawn and go down the mountain, which was quite a climb, and wait for the villagers to come. They'd bring you food, and then you had to climb all the way back up and eat this food before twelve noon. That was quite a problem.

I was with one other monk, a Thai monk, and I thought, 'He's really very good,' and I was quite impressed with him. But when we were on this mountain, he wanted me to teach him English; so I got really angry with him – even felt like murdering him at times!

It was in an area where there was a lot of terrorists and communists, in North-East Thailand. There were helicopters flying overhead sometimes checking us out. Once they came and took me down to the provincial town, wondering whether I was a communist spy.

Then I got violently ill, so ill that they had to carry me down the mountain. I was stuck in a wretched place by a reservoir under a tin roof in the hot season with insects buzzing in and out of my ears and orifices. With horrible food. I nearly died, come to think of it. I almost didn't make it.

But it was during that time in that tin-roof lean-to that a real change took place. I was really despairing and sick and weak and totally depressed, and my mind would fall into these hellish realms, with the terrible heat and discomfort. I felt like I was being cooked; it was like torture.

Vassa: the traditional three-month Rains Retreat undertaken each year in Buddhist monasteries. It is generally a time of heightened attention to matters of training and spiritual instruction.

Then a change came. Suddenly, I just stopped my mind; I refused to get caught in that negativity and I started to practise *anapanasati*. I used the breath to concentrate my mind and things changed very quickly. After that, I recovered my health and it was time to enter the next *Vassa*, so I went back – I'd promised Ajahn Chah I'd go back to Wat Pah Pong for the Vassa – and my robes were all tattered and torn and patched. I looked terrible. When Ajahn Chah saw me, he just burst out laughing. And I was so glad to get back after all that!

I had been trying to practise and what I had wanted were the memories of these insights. I'd forgotten what the insights really were. I was so attached to the idea of working in some kind of ascetic way, like I did the first year, when asceticism really worked. At that time being malnourished and being alone had seemed to provide me with insight, so that for the following several years I kept trying to create the conditions where I would be able to have these fantastic insights.

But the following two or three years seemed to be years of just getting by. Nothing much seemed to happen. I was six months on this mountain before I returned to Wat Pah Pong, just deciding to stay on and follow the insights I had. One of the insights the first year was that I should find a teacher, and that I should learn how to live under a discipline imposed on me by that teacher. So I did that. I realised Ajahn Chah was a good teacher and had a good standard of monastic discipline, so I stayed with him. Those insights that I had were right, but I'd become attached to the memory.

People get very attached to all these special things, like meditation retreats and courses where everything is under control, and everything is organised and there is total silence. Then, even though you do have insight, reflectiveness is not always there because one is assuming that to have these insights you need those conditions.

Actually, insight is more and more a matter of *living* insightfully. It's not just that you have insight *sometimes*, but more and more as you reflect on Dhamma, then everything is insightful. You see insightfully into life as it's happening to you. As soon as you think you have to have special conditions for it, and you're not aware of that, then you're going to create all sorts of complexities about your practice.

So I developed letting go: to not concern myself with attaining or achieving anything. I decided to make little achievements possible by learning to be a little more patient, a little more humble, and a little more generous. I decided to develop this: rather than go out of my way to control and manipulate the environment with the intention of setting myself up in the hope of getting high. It became apparent, through reflection, that the attachment to the insights was the problem. The insights were valid insights, but there was attachment to the memory.

Then the insight came that you let go of all your insights. You don't attach to them. You just keep letting go of all the insights you have because otherwise they become memories, and then memories are conditions of the mind and, if you attach to them, they can only take you to despair.

In each moment it's as it is. With *anapanasati*, one inhalation, at this moment, is *this* way. It's not like yesterday's inhalation was. You're not thinking of yesterday's inhalation and yesterday's exhalation while you're doing the one now. You're with it completely, as it is; so you establish that. The reflective ability is based on establishing your awareness in the way it is *now* rather than having some idea of what you'd like to get, and then trying to get it in the here and now. Trying to get yesterday's blissful feeling in the here and now means you're not aware of the way it is now. You're not with it. Even with *anapanasati*, if you're doing it with the hope of getting the result that you had yesterday, that will make it impossible for that result to ever happen.

Last winter, Venerable Vipassi was meditating in the shrine room and someone was making quite distracting noises. Talking to Venerable Vipassi about it, I was quite impressed, because he said first he felt annoyed and then he decided the noises would be part of the practice. So, he opened his mind to the meditation hall with everything in it – the noises, the silence, the whole thing. That's wisdom, isn't it? If the noise is something you can stop – like a door banging in the wind – go close the door. If there's something you have control over, you can do that.

But much of life you have no control over. You have no right to ask everything to be silent for 'my' meditation. When there is reflectiveness, instead of having a little mind that has to have total silence and special conditions, you have a big mind that can contain the whole of it: the noises, the disruptions, the silence, the bliss, the restlessness, the pain. The mind is all-embracing rather than specialising on a certain refinement in consciousness. Then you develop flexibility because you can concentrate your mind.

This is where wisdom is needed for real development. It's through wisdom that we develop it, not through will-power or controlling or manipulating environmental conditions; getting rid of the things we don't want and trying to set ourselves up so that we can follow this desire to achieve and attain.

Desire is insidious. When we are aware that our intention is to attain some state, that's a desire, isn't it? So we let it go. If we are sitting here, even with a desire to attain the first *jhana*, we recognise that that desire is going to be the very thing that's going to prevent the fulfilment. So we let go of the desire, which doesn't mean not to do *anapanasati*, but to change the attitude to it.

So what can we do now? Develop mindfulness of one inhalation. Most of us can do that; most human beings have enough concentration to be concentrated from the beginning of an inhalation to the end of it. But even if your concentration span is so weak you can't even make it to the end, that's all right. At least you can get to the middle, maybe. That's better than if you gave up totally or never tried at all, isn't it? Because at least you're composing the mind for one second, and that's the beginning: to learn to compose and collect the mind around one thing, like the breath, and sustain it just for the length of one inhalation; if not, then half an inhalation, or a quarter, or whatever. At least you have started, and you must try to develop a mind that's glad at just being able to do that much, rather than being critical because you haven't attained the first *jhana,* or the fourth.

If meditation becomes another thing you have to do, and you feel guilty if you don't live up to your resolutions, then you start pushing yourself without an awareness of what you're doing. Then life does get quite dreary and depressing. But if you are putting that skilful kind of attention into your daily life, you'll find so much of daily life very pleasant – which you may not notice if you are caught in your compulsions and obsessions. If we act with compulsiveness it becomes a burden, a grind. Then we drag ourselves around doing what we have to do in a heedless and negative way. But being able to be in the countryside – the trees, the fields, we have this time for a retreat — we can sit and walk; we don't have a lot to do. The morning chanting, the evening chanting can be extremely pleasant for us, when we're open to it. People are offering the food. The meal is quite a lovely thing. People are eating mindfully and quietly. When we're doing it out of habit and compulsion, then it gets to be a drag.

And a lot of things that are quite pleasant in themselves are no longer pleasant. We can't enjoy them when we're coming from compulsiveness, heedlessness, and ambition. Those are the kinds of driving forces that destroy the joy and the wonder of our lives.

Sustaining your attention on the breathing really develops awareness but when you get lost in thought or restlessness, that's all right too. Don't drive yourself. Don't be a slave driver or beat yourself with a whip and drive yourself in a nasty way. Lead, guide and train yourself; leading onward, guide yourself rather than driving and forcing yourself. Nibbana is a subtle realisation of non-grasping. You can't drive yourself to Nibbana. That's the sure way of never realising it. It's here and now, so if you're driving yourself to Nibbana, you're always going far away from it, driving right over it.

It's pretty heavy, sometimes, to burn up attachments in our mind. The Holy Life is a holocaust, a total burning, a burning up of self, of ignorance. The purity that comes from the holocaust is like a diamond; something that went through such fires that all that was left was purity. And so in our life here there has to be this willingness to burn away the self-views, the opinions, the desires, the restlessness, the greed; all of it, the whole of it, so that there's nothing but purity remaining. Then when there is purity, there is nobody, no thing, there's *that*, the 'suchness'.

And let go of *that*. More and more the path is just the simple being here and now, being with the way things are. There's nowhere to go, nothing to do, nothing to become, nothing to get rid of. Because of the holocaust, there is no ignorance remaining; there is purity, clarity and intelligence.

STILLNESS AND
RESPONSE

When we began the retreat, I asked you to accept the whole of what happens within the next two months. Make your intention not just to have the kind of retreat that you would like, but to open yourself to the possibility of whatever arises. Psychologically, this prepares us for the way life moves and changes. When we set our mind trying to make life into what we want, then we are always feeling frustrated when it does not go quite the way we would like. So try changing the attitude to one of acceptance, and willingness to look at and understand experiences rather than just trying to get rid of them.

You're developing this practice of stillness, the stillness which is everywhere, whether you are in a group or alone. In order to be with the silence, we have to *realise* the stillness, the silence. In other words, be that way – be still and silent.

If one just follows the restless sensations of the body and the proliferations of the mind, then of course, silence is impossible. It can even be a threatening experience because one is so identified with the agitation and restlessness of the sensory realm, and endlessly seeking to get born into it.

The emphasis now is to recognise that restlessness for what it is, to no longer follow it, but to train oneself towards calm. It doesn't mean just to suppress the bodily formation and persecute it, but to train it because these bodies need to be trained with kindness. If you brutalise animals, they are not very nice, are they? They are just frightened, untrustworthy, miserable creatures. To train an animal does not mean you just pamper it, but you guide it. It is the same with your own body. Your body needs to be respected and guided not to follow its restless energy and habits.

But it does not mean you should deny it everything either. A trainer needs to be someone who is both kind and firm, not stubborn or brutal. Not kind in the sense of giving in to everything – because that is not really being kind – but caring, being concerned, having the right amount of interest. The proper attitude towards your own body and mind.

How to calm the body? One way is through 'sweeping meditation', in which you 'sweep' your attention through the body, concentrating on the sensations in the body as you do so. The body needs to be noticed and accepted for what it is. So we bring into consciousness even the tensions, unpleasant sensations and sensation-less parts of the body. By doing that, going from the top of the head to the soles of the feet and back up again, the body will feel relaxed. It's a very healthy meditation, and it will help to train the mind not to be caught up in conceptual proliferation and endless wandering.

Then, as these formations start to calm down, we begin to feel much more aware of the silence of mind. We can abide in that emptiness more and more, where there is no self, just the present moment as it is. The stillness and silence is ever-present wherever we are, no matter what condition we happen to be in.

You can abide in emptiness by just standing among the barren trees of winter and looking at them without creating anything onto them. One can feel a sense of perfect calm and contentment with just being still and silent like the trees. Maybe our egos might say: 'Well I do not want to become like a tree. I want to express my true inner creativity, my unique personality.' We listen to the inner voices that complain and grumble, the wanting-to-become-something, that which stands out or exists. But we are not feeding these creatures, we are letting them go and moving towards the stillness and the silence.

This word 'existence' means 'to stand forth'. Something that doesn't exist doesn't stand forth. So when we say 'non-existing', we are not talking about killing ourselves and no longer being alive but no longer following the desire to stand out, to become something, to be separate. Now that sounds like a real nihilistic view: 'Ajahn Sumedho does not want to exist! Oh, poor man, needs to go to a psychiatrist.' But non-existence does not mean we do not want to have any personalities, that we just want to become dreary boring people. That is not it. It is the ability to abide in the subtlety of just being aware, open and sensitive without being caught in the delusions of trying to become something else or stand out in some way. It is just realising the peace of non-existence – because non-existence is peaceful. And when there is non-existence and emptiness, there is the knowing, the brightness, the wisdom, awareness, clarity, enlightenment. Things are as they are, the suchness, as-is-ness.

In the West, the emphasis is on being special, a unique individual, a child of God. This attitude is very much supported by culture and religion. There are the 'chosen people of God', the sects that feel that they have been called by Jesus (and all the rest haven't); and they are the ones who are going to make it and live in an eternal paradise.

But with all these views of being special, of being an individual, all those self-views – what happens to you? From my own experience, the result of all of this was suffering. There seemed to be a tremendous investment in having a sizzling and unique personality. Sometimes I used to think, 'Wait a minute, maybe I don't a have very nice personality. Maybe I don't have *any* personality.' There was so much anxiety, frustration, jealousy and fear. You didn't want to be a failure, didn't want to be a mediocrity, to be the 'ordinary guy'. It was very painful to be always caught in that desire to become somebody. And as long as one has that desire, then one is always going to fear that you'll become something that's not very good – because fear and desire go together.

At first, this path may seem a bit hopeless. Sometimes the tendencies and habits of a lifetime towards becoming and emphasising yourself as an individual personality are so strong that you feel you should not be that way – you should try to be nobody.

But trying to be nobody is still being somebody. What I am suggesting is not to become nobody but to realise the Truth of mind. Then you can abide in Truth, where you feel most at ease and peaceful, rather than in this endless round of existence in which you're always seeking to be reborn again. In all levels of existence, you'll never find contentment. They never satisfy, not even the best of them. The most blissful conditioned states, the *jhanas*, are still unsatisfactory for us. The Buddha made it very clear that all forms of human happiness and worldly success are really terribly disappointing because they can only temporarily gratify us. And the moment when that gratification is gone, we are caught in the same process of seeking again to be reborn, to become something else, to find another moment of happiness. Life becomes so wearisome.

To live with a body with the right attitude, begin to accept it as it is, and all that it might have right and wrong in it, whether it is young or old, male or female, strong or weak. This is the path to true peacefulness. Do not seek to identify with your body or try to make it into something else. When we know Truth, then at the right times we can be special according to time and place, without it becoming an attachment. One feels one can manifest and disappear according to what is needed. I am not saying that one should just stand among the trees for the rest of one's life. One can be something that is useful and helpful to others – but it is not a permanent role that one is trying to hold onto and defend any more. So one begins to feel a sense of freedom and ease.

When I was young I was very self-conscious – to say something in public was absolutely terrifying for me. Even when I was in the Navy, just having to raise my voice to say, 'Aye aye sir !' in public in a roll call would have me shaking because of self-consciousness. Then I became a schoolteacher. Teaching 8-9 year old Chinese kids in N. Borneo for a couple of years – that wasn't such a threat. But then becoming a monk in Thailand and eventually having to give talks to Thai people in Thai . . .! All this self-consciousness became apparent: the highs you'd get when you felt you'd given a good talk and everybody says : 'You're really good, Sumedho, you can give good Dhamma.' Then sometimes I would give a really stupid talk and think, 'I don't want to give another talk, ever again. I didn't become a monk to give talks.'

But the idea was to keep watching this. Luang Por* Chah would always encourage me to keep aware of the pride, the conceit, the embarrassment and the self-consciousness that I would feel. And fortunately in Thailand, the people are such that they're just grateful for a monk giving a talk. Even if it's not a very good talk, it doesn't seem to upset them very much. They still seem quite grateful about it. So that made it quite easy. One time, at a Kathina* ceremony where we had to sit up all night, Ajahn Chah said, 'Sumedho, you

*Luang Por: The Thai term translates as 'Venerable Father', although the English does not convey the mixture of affection and respect that it signifies. It is used in addressing an elderly monk.
*Kathina: a ceremony held at the end of a Vassa in which lay people make offerings to the monastery.

have to give a talk for three hours tonight.' And up till that time I'd only talked for half an hour. *That* was a strain – but *three hours !!* And he *knew*.

With Ajahn Chah, I always felt that if he said something, I'd do it. So I sat up on the high seat and talked for three hours. I had to sit there and watch people get up and leave; and I had to sit there and watch people just lie down on the floor and sleep in front of me. And at the end of the three hours, there were still a few polite old ladies left sitting there!

That wasn't Ajahn Chah saying, 'O.K. Sumedho, go in there and bowl them over with some scintillating stuff! Entertain them, really sock it to them!' I began to realise that what he wanted me to do was to be able to look at this self-consciousness, the posing, the pride, the conceit, the grumbling, the lazy, the 'not-wanting-to-be-bothered', the wanting to please, the wanting to entertain, the wanting to get approval.

All these have come up during these talks of the past fifteen years. But the meditation is one in which, more and more, one feels a real understanding of the suffering of a self-view. And then through that insight, one realises the abiding in emptiness.

Whenever Ajahn Chah used to give a talk, he'd sit there and close his eyes and then he'd start talking – and what would come out would be appropriate to time and place. He said to never prepare a talk – he didn't care if they were interesting or not – just to let them come. And when there's non-existence, no self anymore, there are none of the problems we build out of 'What do people think of me? What do people say about me?' Or the rebellion – 'They can think what they want, I don't care!' (But you do really, don't you? Otherwise you wouldn't have to say that, would you?)

Sometimes personalities manifest, at the appropriate times. As you talk, you manifest your personality. Now maybe you are still caught up in being a person in your own mind. But these are merely conditions that arise and cease and come out of fear and desire. When there is emptiness, personality still operates – it does not mean that we are exactly OK!, like bees in a hive. There are still the myriad differences of character and personality that can manifest to be charming or whatever. But there is no delusion about them – there is no suffering.

For example, when Ajahn Chah first visited England, he was invited to a certain woman's home for a vegetarian meal. She obviously had put a lot of effort into creating the most delicious kinds of food. She was bustling about offering this food and looking very enthusiastic. Ajahn Chah was sitting there assessing the situation, and then suddenly he said, 'This is the most delicious and wonderful meal I have ever had!'

That comment was really something, because in Thailand monks are not suppose to comment on the food. And yet Luang Por suddenly manifested this charming character that complimented a woman who needed to be complimented because that made her feel so happy. He had a feeling for the time and place, for the person he was with, for what would be kind. So he could step out of the designated role of what is supposed to be according to a tradition, and manifest in ways that are appropriate.

Now that shows wisdom and the ability to respond to a situation; not to be just rigidly bound within a convention that blinds you. That was a manifestation – and a disappearance too, because I have never heard him do that again.

The empty mind is an abiding in ease, where there is no self, no fear or desire to be deluded with. And yet there is the ability to respond out of compassion and kindness to the present situation in a suitable way. It is strange, isn't it? Compare the goal of Nibbana, of non-existence, with that of becoming the best person in the whole world, the strongest or the most beautiful. Worldly values are about having power, beauty, wealth – but they all have their opposites, don't they? Success is always attached to failure, happiness is always attached to unhappiness, praise is always attached to blame. Good fortune to bad fortune. So if you choose the worldly values of wealth, power, success and praise, you are going to get the others along with them because they are like two sides of the same coin. You can't separate the one from the other. Worldly values are never really going to allow you to feel at ease.

The world is an unsafe place, it's not peaceful. And it's not where we really belong. You only begin to understand and realise peace through emptiness, non-existence, non-self. And this is not annihilation, but enlightenment, freedom, true peace, true knowledge.

Reflections on Sharing Blessings

Now let us chant the verses of sharing and aspiration.

Through the goodness that arises from my practice,
May my spiritual teachers and guides of great virtue,
My mother, my father and my relatives,
The sun and the moon,
And all virtuous leaders of the world –
May the highest gods and evil forces;
Celestial beings, guardian spirits of the Earth
And the Lord of Death;
May those who are friendly, indifferent or hostile;
May all beings receive the blessings of my life.
May they soon attain the threefold bliss
And realise the Deathless.
    Through the goodness that arises from my practice,
And through this act of sharing,
May all desires and attachments quickly cease
And all harmful states of mind.
Until I realise Nibbana,
In every kind of birth,
May I have an upright mind
With mindfulness and wisdom, austerity and vigour
May the forces of delusion not take hold
nor weaken my resolve.
    The Buddha is my excellent refuge
Unsurpassed is the protection of the Dhamma
The Solitary Buddha is my noble Lord
The Sangha is my supreme support
Through the supreme power of all these,
May darkness and delusion be dispelled.

TURNING TOWARDS
EMPTINESS

By reflecting, you bring into consciousness the state of conditions as they happen to be now. Having been born we're now at this age, feeling this way, at this time and in this place. That's the way it is. That cannot be changed by us. It's just the inevitability of birth that this is the way it is now.

And with that reflection, you get a *perspective* on the way it is rather than the *reaction* to the way it is. If you don't reflect, then you just react to the way it is.

If you're feeling happy you get high, 'I want to be a monk for the rest of my life and devote myself to the Dhamma. Dhamma is the way for me. The only way, the true way . . .' and you go out and bore people with a harangue on the importance of Buddhism in the world because you're high and you feel positive and confident. Even that feeling of being inspired and confident and full of faith and devotion and all these kinds of things – that's the way it is. One can feel a lot of faith and confidence in what one is doing.

But also one can feel the opposite: one loses faith, one feels that it is a waste of time, 'I've wasted my life. It's of no value, I haven't gotten anywhere. It hasn't done anything for me. I don't believe in it anymore, I'm fed up with it.' And one can feel indifference: 'It's all right, don't know what else to do. Better than working in a factory.' If that's the way you're feeling now – either extreme or just indifference – that's the way it is.

So just notice when you're feeling tremendous energy and feeling positive, or when there's a lack of it and you're too critical. When you're depressed and when you're not feeling very well, or when you're tired, it's hard to arouse the inspired feeling. In those circumstances, you tend to pick up what's wrong with things very quickly. The way somebody walks across a room can really irritate you. Somebody blows their nose too hard – and oh, that's disgusting! But when you are feeling full of inspiration and devotion, you just don't care about the faults of this or that, you're just caught up in this feeling of devotion and faith. These perceptions are to be reflected on as the way it is now. It has to be this way, because it can't be any other way at this moment. We feel like this, we feel tired or invigorated or whatever – this is the way it is.

These are the results of having been born and living our lives and being subject to changing conditions of sensuality. Then note, really note, what you add to the existing conditions. In all-night sittings, you may feel sleepy or tired; note what you put on to that feeling. Note the feeling itself, but maintain a posture rather than just react to feeling tired by trying to annihilate the feeling by following it and sinking into lethargy.

When you're really convinced that you're so tired there's nothing you can do about it, and even pulling your body straight is something that seems totally impossible, hold it up straight for a length of time. Observe, and learn how much energy it takes to hold a body up.

How much energy does it take to stop the thinking process? Have you ever noticed that? 'Just can't stop thinking' – the mind goes on and on. 'Can't stop, what can I do?' 'I don't know how to stop thinking – it keeps going. I can't stop it. . . .' I know the problem because I've always had a problem with a mind that just seemed to be endlessly thinking about something. And the desire to stop thinking and the effort to get rid of it creates the conditions for more thinking!

It takes effort to do it, not just thinking about it. I remember one time an Australian Abhidhamma fanatic came to Wat Pah Pong. This man had a mission – when Westerners get into Abhidhamma they become like born-again Christians – but he didn't know how to meditate; he didn't believe that meditation worked, and he figured it all out with his Abhidhamma concepts. He felt that you couldn't stop thinking. He said, 'You're always thinking and you can't stop thinking'. And I said, 'But you can stop thinking'. And he said, 'No you can't...', and I said, 'I've just stopped thinking...', and he said, 'No you haven't!'

Pointless to go on talking to someone like that. You have to be alert to know when you are not thinking, so you take an actual thought like 'I can't stop thinking', and you deliberately think that. This is what I did, because I was a habitual, obsessive thinker.

So instead of trying to stop thinking, if you are averse to it, then go to the other extreme and deliberately think something. And watch yourself deliberately thinking so that it's not just a wandering thought process in which your mind goes round and round in circles.

Use your wisdom faculty; deliberately think something, some thought that is completely neutral and uninteresting, like 'I am a human being'. Then deliberately think it, but observe the space before you're thinking, and then deliberately say, 'I am a human being'. Then you note the end of it the moment you stop thinking. Pay attention to before and after the thought rather than to the thought itself – just hold that attention to where there is no thought. Investigate the space *around* the thought, the space where the thought comes and goes, rather than thinking.

Then you're aware of an empty mind, where there's just awareness but no thought. That may last just for a second because you start grasping, so you just have to keep being more aware by again thinking something. With practice you can use even very unpleasant thoughts. For example, you might have strong emotional feelings of 'I'm no good, I'm worthless' and this can be an obsession. In some people's minds it can become a background to their lives. So you try thinking: 'I shouldn't think that. Venerable Sumedho says I'm good. But I *know* I'm no good.' However, if you take that obsession and use it as a conscious thought: 'I am no good', you start seeing the space around it. And it no longer sounds so absolute, does it? When it becomes obsessive it sounds absolute, it's infallible, the honest truth, the real truth: 'This is what I really am, I'm no good.' But when you actually take it out of the context of obsession – and deliberately intentionally think it – you're seeing it objectively.

That sense of 'me' and 'mine' is just a habit of the mind; it's not the truth. If you really take the 'I/I am' and look at it objectively, that *feeling* created by that 'I am' and 'I am this way' or 'I should be/should not be' is very different than when you're just reacting.

In contemplating the Four Noble Truths, you have the truth of suffering; its arising; its cessation and then the Path. You can't know the Path and the way out of suffering until you are aware of where everything ceases – in the mind itself. The mind is still vital and alert even when there is no thought in it; but if you don't notice that, then you believe you are always thinking. That's the way it seems.

You only conceive of yourself when you're thinking because you're identified with memory and the sense of 'I am' or 'I am not'. That 'yourself' is very much a conditioned, programmed perception in the mind. As long as you believe in that perception and never question it, then you will always believe that you are an obsessive thinker. . . and you shouldn't be *this* way or shouldn't feel *that* way and you shouldn't worry – but you do, and you're a hopeless case and so it goes on from one thing to another.

So the 'I am' is just a perception really – it arises in the mind and it ceases in the mind. When it ceases, note that cessation of thought. Make that cessation, that empty mind, a 'sign' rather than just creating more things in the emptiness. You can get refined states of consciousness fixing on refined objects – as in *samatha* meditation practices that emphasise calming the mind – but with the contemplation of the Noble Truths, you're using the wisdom faculty to note where everything ceases.

And yet when the mind is empty, the senses are still all right. It's not like being in a trance, totally oblivious to everything; your mind is open, empty – or you might call it whole, complete, bright. Then you can take anything: ...like a fearful thought. You can take that and deliberately think it and see it as just another condition of the mind, rather than as a psychological problem. It arises, it ceases; there's nothing in it, nothing in any thought. It's just a movement in the mind and therefore it's not a person. You *make* it personal by attaching to it, believing it: 'And I'm such a hopeless case, I know I can never be enlightened, after all the things I've done; the stupid things. And I'm so selfish and I've made so many mistakes. I know there's no hope for me.' *All that arises and ceases in the mind!*

Believing is grasping, isn't it? 'I know what I am and I know I'm no good.' You believe that, and that's what grasping is. You *create* that belief, so the mind goes on in that way. And you can find all kinds of proof that you're no good – you can even start getting paranoid: 'Everybody knows that I'm no good, too. Venerable Sucitto yesterday, he walked by and I just *knew* that he knows I'm no good. Then this morning I came in the hall and Sister Rocana looked at me a little bit strange – she knows!'

So through belief you can see and interpret everything that people do in a personal way, as if they've all been condemning and judging you – that's paranoia, isn't it?

Even the most beautiful thoughts and aspirations as well as the most evil and nasty arise and cease in the mind. Now don't misunderstand me; I'm not saying good and evil thoughts are the same. They have the same characteristic of arising and ceasing, that's all. In other respects, they're different. Good thoughts are good thoughts, evil thoughts are evil thoughts! So I'm not saying it's all right to think evil thoughts, but I am pointing beyond the quality of the thought: love and hate arise and cease in the mind. In this perspective, you're going to the reflective mind where most people are totally unaware. People are generally only aware of themselves as a personality or an emotion or a thought – in other words, as a condition.

For practice, don't worry about the qualities that go through the mind: how wonderful, interesting, beautiful, ugly, nasty or neutral they might be. We're not investigating qualities, or denying the quality of any thought, but just noting the way it is. Then you just leave it alone so it ceases. You create a thought, put it into the mind deliberately and let it go. To let go doesn't mean you push it away: you leave the thought alone, you're aware of it during the whole time; the moment before the thought and the interstices and the ending.

The space around thought – we don't notice that very much, do we? It is just like the space in this room, I have to call your attention to it. Now what does it take to be aware of the space in this room? You have to be alert. With the *objects* in the room you don't have to be alert, you can just be attracted or repelled: 'I don't like that, I like this.' You can just react to the quality of beauty and ugliness, whether it pleases or displeases you. It's our habit, isn't it? Our life tends to be reaction to pleasure and pain, beauty and ugliness. So we see beauty and we say, 'Oh, look at that! Isn't it absolutely fantastic?' or you think, 'Oh, disgusting!'

But the beautiful objects and the ugly ones are all in the *space* and to notice space you withdraw your attention from the objects of beauty and ugliness. Of course they're still there, you needn't throw them out; you don't have to tear down the building so that we can have a space here. But if you don't concentrate with love or hate on what's in that room, if you don't make anything out of it, your attention withdraws from the objects and you notice the space.

So we have a perspective on space in a room like this. You can reflect on that. Anyone can come and go in this space. The most beautiful, the most ugly, saint and sinner, can come and go in this space and the space is never harmed or ruined or destroyed by the objects that come and go in this space.

The mind works on the same principle. But if you're not used to seeing the spaciousness of your mind, you are not aware of the space that the mind really is. So you're unaware of the emptiness of the mind because you're always attached to an idea or an opinion or mood.

With insight meditation, you're reflecting on the five *khandhas* – on the body (*rupa*), feelings (*vedana*), perception (*sañña*), mind formations (*sankhara*) and sense consciousness (*viññana*). We may want to get rid of them, but that is another condition, another *sankhara* that we create. So we investigate them until they no longer delude us, and allow them to cease in the empty mind. When you think, 'My body's still here – how does it cease? It's still here, isn't it?' Consider that the body will live its lifespan, since it's been born and it will disappear when its kammic force ends.

What happened to Napoleon? What happened to the Queen of Sheba? And Confucius and Lao Tzu and Marie Antoinette, Beethoven and Bach? They're memories in our minds; they're just perceptions in people's minds now. *But that's all they ever were anyway, even when their bodies were alive!*

'Venerable Sumedho' is a perception in the mind – in my mind it's a perception, in your mind it's a perception. Right now the perception of it is, 'Venerable Sumedho is alive and kicking.' When the body dies, then the perception changes to, 'Venerable Sumedho is dead.' That's all, isn't it? The perception of death is there along with the name Sumedho, where now it is alive and kicking. So as you experience it, the body is a perception in the mind that arises – and ceases in the empty mind.

With this realisation of the empty mind, you can develop the Eightfold Path very skilfully. The Eightfold Path is based on right understanding, and that is the understanding of cessation.

BEYOND BELIEF

From the appearance of the five *khandhas* – *rupa*, *vedana*, *sañña*, *sankhara*, *viññana* – and the unquestioned belief that they are oneself – it always seems that the mind is in the body, doesn't it? To most people, if you say 'Where's your mind?' they will point to their head or their hearts.

But if you investigate the way things are, following the teachings of the Buddha, then you begin to realise that the body is in the mind. Mind is really what comes first – the body is just the receptor. It's a sensitive receptor, like a radio, or radar, or something like that. It's not a person, it's not anything other than an instrument.

When that view of being within the five *khandhas* is seen through and let go of, then there's a realisation of what we can call 'deathlessness', immortality. These words imply 'beyond the conditioned', and the ability to conceive the deathless is impossible, isn't it? You can point at a word like 'deathless', or 'immortal,' or 'unconditioned,' but beyond that there's no more that you can say about it because words are themselves conditioned and mortal. Words, concepts, perceptions, conceptions are only appropriate to the conditioned world. As long as you're attached to thoughts and to concepts, to views and opinions, no matter how intelligent and altruistic these views might be, that very attachment will bind you to the conditioned realm – you just keep being reborn into it. You keep searching for the unconditioned in the conditioned, you keep looking for God in the mortal condition, in the changing nature of sensory consciousness, only to feel totally frustrated and disappointed. Then you have to support that 'soul view' by a kind of stubborn belief.

Beliefs don't change, do they? You can believe in exactly the same things you believed in when you were five when you are fifty! That belief is the grasping of a perception.

There are some beliefs that are very nice, pretty and sentimental. The romantic and sentimental view of life presents a pretty

101

picture that we can still believe in even when we're 80! When my Gran died at 75, she still had a 16-year-old girl's emotional development. When she died, she had a boyfriend called 'Hercules Cavalier' who was her gigolo! She still had the same kind of romantic longings as when she was a 16-year-old girl! So even though at 75 she was a physical wreck, yet the mind was still attached to those pretty pictures of youth.

We assume and believe, and never question the prejudice and fixed views that we're grasping, that we never change. They don't change; we keep re-affirming the same old things over and over. And that's why so many political problems arise: it's because so many people hold on to political views rather than try to be aware of the needs of a particular time and place.

How much violence and meanness and nastiness is done in the name of property alone! And boundaries: 'This is my land, get off my land.' You see it all the time, in the endless border problems of countries. Then the meanness of heart, not wanting to let people in, – or not wanting to let people out! – because of the unquestioned belief, 'This is my house/my family/my wife/my husband/my children, my, my, my. . . .'

Over the course of twenty years of meditation, I can see that a lot of attachments, obsessions and tendencies have fallen away because of allowing things to cease. The process has been one of letting things go rather than believing, grasping, and becoming reborn in endless thought patterns and desires. When we view life as just a passage, then we are not going to hang on to it. We're not going to become mean and selfish because we realise that nothing is worth holding on to – any material wealth, property, status, or worldly values, or anything. There is nothing worth bothering with that much because it is not really ours anyway. Of course, we can *believe* that it's ours. But in actual investigation, in looking into the way the mind actually is, we see that nothing really belongs to us anyway – there's nobody to own anything!

Now with the reflection of the body being in the mind, this grasping changes. You have to start contemplating what the mind really is – because your body's certainly not in your brain, is it? It's ridiculous! Nor is your blood-pumping heart. They're in your body.

I was standing out this evening and looking at the dusk, at the trees, the barren trees on the borders of Amaravati, just contemplating that the trees are in the mind, and that trees are conscious.

There's a certain level of consciousness in all life, in the fact that there is receptivity to the environment; and trees are very receptive to the environment they are in. One begins to change the perception of mind to one of a consciousness that pervades everything. Then it's not just a human mind, there's something more to it. But in Buddhism it is never named, you never try to form a concept about it. Instead you contemplate the totality, the whole sensitivity, the sensory realm and what it is really about. And this we have to contemplate from our own ability to be conscious and to feel but not see it in terms of 'me' and 'mine' – 'I feel these things but nobody else does', or 'Only human beings do and animals don't', or 'Only mammals do, and reptiles don't', or 'Only the animal and insect kingdoms do but not the plants.' Consciousness does not imply thought but it does imply receptivity to what is impinging, to what comes to it. We begin to see that consciousness is a vital, changing universal system; it's like a plenum, it's full with all possibilities, all potentials of form, of what can be created. Whatever we can think of, we can see that in terms of the human ability to imagine, through which we can create all kinds of fantasies that come into material form.

But the greatest, most profound and meaningful human potential is overlooked by most people, and this is the ability to understand the truth of the way it is, to see the Dhamma, to be free from all delusions.

When you are contemplating reality, begin to reflect on where there is no self. Whenever there is the cessation of self, there is just clarity, knowing, and contentedness – you feel at ease and balanced. It takes a while to be able to give up all the striving , and restless tendencies of the body and mind. But, in moments, that will cease; and there's a real clarity, contented peacefulness. And in that also, there is no self, no 'me' and 'my'. You can contemplate that.

We must recognise that we have to learn through being totally humbled, by never succeeding at anything we are doing in this meditation, by never being successful, never getting what we want; if we do get what we want, we lose it right away. We have to be totally humbled to where any form of self-view is relinquished willingly, graciously, humbly. That's why, in meditation, the more it comes from will-power based on a self-view and on 'me achieving and attaining,' then of course, you can only expect failure and despair because this is not a worldly pursuit. In worldly situations, if you are clever and strong, gifted and have opportunities, and the conditions are there, you can barge your way through and become a great success, can't you. With the survival of the fittest you can manage to get above and destroy the competition – you can be a winner.

But even a winner, on the worldly plane, is still going to be a failure, because if you win something you are going to lose something too. Winning and losing go together. So winning is never as wonderful as it might look, is it? It is more the anticipation of winning. If you've actually won something – so what? You have a moment of elation, maybe – 'I'm a winner!' – but then, 'Now what do I do? What do I have to win next?'

Winning, worldly goals, and worldly values are really not going to satisfy us, so if we apply that same attitude toward the religious life, it's just not going to work. We just feel a sense of total despair, helplessness – because we need that, we need to lose everything, to let go of everything, all hope, all expectations, all demands, to where we can just be with the way things are, and not expect or demand them to be otherwise.

The practice of the Buddha is to accept life as it is. This is the way it is. Our reflection as mendicants is that we have enough to eat, robes to wear, a roof over our heads and medicine for illness. The Dhamma and Vinaya are taught. It is good enough; therefore we begin to say, 'It's all right, I'm content', and not make problems or dwell on the irritations and frustrations that we find here.

I find myself now much more at ease with letting life be as it is here in Amaravati, and with the way things are – with the weather, with the people, with the country. Not to compare it, not to judge it, but to be grateful for the opportunity, and to be accepting of whatever is. And it isn't all that easy, believe me, because I can be quite critical too, and fussy. There's also a strong sense of responsibility in wanting to make things right, and work properly – not just wanting nice things for myself, but wanting to make everything right and good for everyone else. I can really be caught up with responsibility, being an Ajahn and an abbot and all that – you try to set a good example. You get obsessed with that. I always felt I had to be a kind of cardboard monk, a plastic Sumedho Bhikkhu! If you saw anything other than the perfect smile and the stereotype presence, then you'd lose all faith in the Dhamma!

So we begin to let go of that, even the altruistic tendencies of feeling responsible. It doesn't mean that one is irresponsible, but one is letting go of those ideas, those views that we can be so blinded by. They might be very good views, but if you grasp them you can't get beyond them.

In living the Holy Life you train yourself to being open and willing to learn from the ups and downs and the way things happen to be – the irritations and problems of community life, and the way things are – rather than resist, avoid and reject life. You give up controlling and manipulating, and trying to change the world and make it into what you want it to be. One has to give up, let go of that kind of inclination, and abide in the knowing, in the mindfulness.

In practice, just notice if you're trying too hard. If you've got the view that you have to stay awake, that can make you compulsive: the 'I have to stay awake' compulsion. Notice if you attach to either extreme, like 'I have to stay awake', or 'It doesn't matter'. You can use one to counterbalance the other; if you tend to think 'It doesn't matter', you need to practise 'I must stay awake', but if you're caught in the 'I must stay awake' compulsion, you can say 'It doesn't matter, let go'. Neither one is a fixed position; they're just skilful means to find the middle, the place of balance. You don't come in here and say, 'It doesn't matter, let go, that's my practice', then fall over asleep because it doesn't matter! 'It's all Dhamma, sleeping Buddha, awake Buddha.'

There's also the compulsive 'I don't want to fall asleep, it matters so much to stay awake! Ajahn Sumedho says, "You come here to be awake, not to fall asleep!" ' *Then* one can become caught in the compulsion to be awake. The knowing is the knowing of what's driving us, what we're attached to, where that attachment is; and it does take patience to see it – and to acknowledge it.

One of the factors of enlightenment is devotion, an emotional sweetness and joyfulness. We tend to want everything on the level of intellectual concepts, but we also need to humble ourselves towards the joy and sweetness of loving the Buddha, the Dhamma and Sangha – especially if we find our practice is getting a bit 'dried-up'. This is to advise you not to be frightened of loving and joy, and open-hearted generosity. Human life without this is a dreary desert, isn't it, just like living in a museum. It's all nice and clean with marble corridors, but cold, ordered, catalogued. In museums everything is dusted and put in order, but it's cold!

So religion also gives us this opportunity towards this warmth, the joy, the love, the devotion, the offering, the giving. This is very much a foundation and a necessity for religious life. See our life here in the community as an opportunity to manifest generosity, love and joy, not just as an obsession with looking at our *citta* to see what is moving through it at this moment, seeing that it's *anicca*, *dukkha*, *anatta*. We do that in order to reflect on the way things are, to be free from the illusions or the attachments to love and generosity – because if you attach to concepts of love and generosity then that will also bring you to despair.

For this retreat the lay people have come to give, to help the Sangha. This is their act of love and generosity, and so our appreciation for that act of generosity is our determination to practise, to realise the Dhamma, so that our lives will be a blessing to the lay community.

We can reflect on it in this way, not to take the situation for granted in any way whatsoever; but to allow space for the joy and the gratitude one feels. These qualities help provide the foundation for our own understanding of freedom from delusion.

BEING NOBODY

Try to note the cessation or the ending of things in little ways by paying special attention to the ending of the outbreath. This way, in your daily life, you're noticing the ordinary endings that no-one ever pays attention to. I've found this practice very useful because it's a way of noticing the changing nature of the conditioned realm as one is living one's daily life. As I understand it, it was to these ordinary states of mind that the Buddha was pointing, not to the special highly-developed concentrated states.

The first year that I practised, I was on my own and I could get into highly-developed concentrated states of mind which I really enjoyed. Then I went to Wat Pah Pong, where the emphasis was on the way of life in accordance with Vinaya discipline and a routine. There one always had to go out on alms-round every morning, and do the morning chanting and evening chanting. If you were young and healthy, you were expected to go on these very long alms-rounds – they had shorter ones that the old feeble monks could go on. In those days, I was very vigorous so I was always going on these long, long alms-rounds and then I'd come back tired, then there would be the meal and then in the afternoon we all had chores to do. It was not possible under those conditions to stay in a concentrated state. Most of the day was taken up by daily life routine.

So I got fed up with all this and went to see Luang Por Chah and said, 'I can't meditate here', and he started laughing at me and telling everyone that, 'Sumedho can't meditate here!' I was seeing meditation as this very special experience that I'd had and quite enjoyed and then Luang Por Chah was obviously pointing to the ordinariness of daily life, the getting up, the alms-rounds, the routine work, the chores: the whole thing was for mindfulness. And he didn't seem at all eager to support me in my desires to have strong sensory deprivation experience by not having to do all these little daily tasks. He didn't seem to go along with that; so I ended up having to conform and learn to meditate in the ordinariness of daily life. And in the long run that has been the most helpful.

It has not always been what I *wanted* because one wants the special; one would love to have blazing light and marvellous insights in Technicolor and have incredible bliss and ecstasy and rapture – not be just happy and calm – but over the moon!

But reflecting on life in this human form: it is just like this, it's being able to sit peacefully and get up peacefully and be content with what you have; it's that which makes our life as a daily experience something that is joyful and not suffering. And this is how most of our life can be lived – you can't live in ecstatic states of rapture and bliss and do the dishes, can you? I used to read about the lives of saints that were so caught up in ecstasies they couldn't do anything on any practical level. Even though the blood would flow from their palms and they could do feats that the faithful would rush to look at, when it came to anything practical or realistic they were quite incapable.

And yet when you contemplate the Vinaya discipline itself, it is a training in being mindful. It's about mindfulness with regard to making robes, collecting alms food, eating food, taking care of your kuti; what to do in this situation or that situation. It's all very practical advice about the daily life of a bhikkhu. An ordinary day in the life of Bhikkhu Sumedho isn't about exploding into rapture but getting up and going to the toilet and putting on a robe and bathing and doing this or that; it's just about being mindful while one is living in this form and learning to awaken to the way things are, to the Dhamma.

That's why whenever we contemplate cessation, we're not looking for the end of the universe but just the exhalation of the breath or the end of the day or the end of the thought or the end of the feeling. To notice that means that we have to pay attention to the flow of life – we have to really notice the way it is rather than wait for some kind of fantastic experience of marvellous light descending on us, zapping us or whatever.

Now just contemplate the ordinary breathing of your body. You notice if you're inhaling, that it's easy to concentrate. When you're filling your lungs, you feel a sense of growth and development and strength. When you say somebody's 'puffed up', then they're probably inhaling. It's hard to feel puffed up while you're exhaling. Expand your chest and you have a sense of being somebody big and powerful.

However, when I first started paying attention to exhaling, my mind would wander; exhaling didn't seem as important as inhaling – you were just doing it so that you could get on to the next inhalation.

Now reflect: one can observe breathing, so what is it that can observe? What is it that observes and knows the inhalation and the exhalation – that's not the breathing, is it? You can also observe the panic that comes if you want to catch a breath and you can't; but the observer, that which knows, is not an emotion, not panic-stricken, is not an exhalation or an inhalation. So our refuge in Buddha is being that knowing; being the witness rather than the emotion or the breath or the body.

With the sound of silence*, some people hear fluctuations of sound or a continuous background of sound. So you can contemplate it, you notice that – can you notice it if you put your fingers in your ears? Can you hear it in a place where they are using the chain saw? or when you're doing exercises or when you're in a fraught emotional state? You're using this sound of silence as something to remember to turn to and notice – because it's always present here and now. And there's that which notices it.

There is the desire of the mind to call it something, to have a name for it, have it listed as some kind of attainment or project something on to it. Notice that, the tendency of wanting to make it into something. Somebody said it's probably just the sound of your blood circulating in your ears, somebody else called it 'the cosmic sound', 'the bridge to the Divine.' That sounds nicer than 'the blood in your ears'. It might be the sound of the Cosmos or it might be that you've got an ear disease. But it doesn't have to be anything; it's what it is, it's 'as that.' Whatever it is, it can be used as reflection because when you're with that, there is no sense of self, there is mindfulness, there is the ability to reflect.

So it is more like a straight edge that you can go to, to keep you from going all wobbly. It is something you can use to compose yourself in daily life, when you're putting on your robes, when you're brushing your teeth, when you're closing a door, when you're coming into the meditation hall, when you're sitting down. So much of daily life is just habitual because we aim at what we consider to be the important things of life – like the meditation. So, walking from where you live to the Meditation Hall can be a totally heedless

* See P75 – 78

experience – just a habit – clump, clump, clump, slam bang! Then you sit here for an hour trying to be mindful.

This way you begin to see a way of being mindful, of bringing mindfulness to the ordinary routines and experiences of life. I have a nice little picture in my room that I'm very fond of – of this old man with a coffee mug in his hand, looking out of the window into an English garden with the rain coming down. The title of the picture is 'Waiting.' That's how I think of myself; an old man with my coffee mug sitting there at the window, waiting, waiting. . . watching the rain or the sun or whatever. I don't find that a depressing image but rather a peaceful one. This life is just about waiting, isn't it? We're waiting all the time – so we notice that. We're not waiting *for* anything, but we can be just waiting. And then we respond to the things of life, to the time of day, the duties, the way things move and change, the society we are in. That response isn't from the force of habits of greed, hatred and delusion but it's a response of wisdom and mindfulness.

Now how many of you feel you have a mission in life to perform? It's something you've got to do and some kind of important task that's been assigned to you by God or fate or something. People frequently get caught up in that view of being somebody who has a mission. Who can be just with the way things are, so that it is just the body that grows up, gets old and dies, breathes and is conscious? We can practise, live within the moral precepts, do good, respond to the needs and experiences of life with mindfulness and wisdom – but there's nobody that has to *do* anything. There's nobody with a mission, nobody special, we're not making a person or a saint or an avatar or a tulku or a messiah or Maitreya. Even if you think: 'I'm just a nobody.' even being a nobody is somebody in this life, isn't it? You can be just as proud of being nobody as of being somebody, and just as deluded attached to being nobody. But whatever you happen to believe, that you're a nobody or a somebody or you have a mission or you're a nuisance and a burden to the world or however you might view yourself, then the knowing is there to see the cessation of such a view.

Views arise and cease, don't they? 'I'm somebody, an important person who has a mission in life': that arises and ceases in the mind. Notice the ending of being somebody important or being nobody or whatever – it all ceases, doesn't it? Everything that arises, ceases, so there's a non-grasping of the view of being somebody with a mission or of being nobody. There's the end of that whole mass of suffering – of having to develop something, become somebody, change something, set everything right, get rid of all your defilements or save the world. Even the best ideals, the best thoughts can be seen as *dhammas* that arise and cease in the mind.

Now, you might think that this is a barren philosophy of life because there's a lot more heart and feeling in being somebody who's going to save all sentient beings. People with self-sacrifice who have missions and help others and have something important to do are an inspiration. But when you notice that as *dhamma*, you are looking at the limitations of inspirations and the cessation of it. Then there is the *dhamma* of those aspirations and actions rather than *somebody* who has to become something or has to do something. The whole illusion is relinquished and what remains is purity of mind. Then the response to experience comes from wisdom and purity rather than from personal conviction and mission with its sense of self and other, and all the complications that come from that whole pattern of delusion.

Can you trust that? Can you trust in just letting everything go and cease and not being anybody and not having any mission, not having to becomes anything? Can you really trust in that or do you find it frightening, barren or depressing? Maybe you really want inspiration. 'Tell me everything is all right; tell me you really love me; what I'm doing is right and Buddhism is not just a selfish religion where you get enlightened for your own sake; tell me that Buddhism is here to save all sentient beings. Is that what you're going to do, Venerable Sumedho? Are you really Mahayana or Hinayana?'

What I'm pointing to is what inspiration is as an experience. Idealism: not trying to dismiss it or to judge it in any way but to reflect on it, to know what that is in the mind and how easily we can be deluded by our own ideas and high-minded views. And to see how insensitive, cruel and unkind we can be by the attachment we have to views about being kind and sensitive. This is where it is a real investigation into Dhamma.

I remember in my own experience, I always had the view that I was somebody special in some way; I used to think, 'Well I *must* be a special person. Way back when I was a child I was fascinated by Asia and as soon as I could, I studied Chinese at the university, so

111

surely I *must* have been a reincarnation of somebody who was connected to the Orient.'

But consider this as a reflection: no matter how many signs of being special or previous lives you can remember or voices from God or messages from the Cosmos, whatever – not to deny that or say that those things aren't real – but they're impermanent. They're *anicca, dukkha, anatta.* We're reflecting on them as they really are – what arises ceases: a message from God is something that comes and ceases in your mind, doesn't it? God isn't *always* talking to you continuously unless you want to consider the silence the voice of God. Then it doesn't really say anything does it? We can call it anything – we can call it the voice of God or the divine or the ringing of the cosmos or blood in your ear drums. But whatever it is, it can be used for mindfulness and reflection – that's what I'm pointing to, how to use these things without making them into something.

Then the missions we have are responses, not to experiences that we have in our lives – they're not personal anymore, it's no longer me, Sumedho Bhikkhu, with a mission as if I'm specially chosen from above, more so than any of you. It's not that any more. That whole manner of thinking and perceiving is relinquished. And whether or not I do save the world and thousands of beings or help the poor in the slums of Calcutta or help to cure all lepers and do all kinds of good works – it's not from the delusion of being a person, it's a natural response from wisdom.

This I trust; this is what *saddha* it is – is a faith in the Buddha's word. *Saddha*: it's a real trust and confidence in Dhamma; in just waiting and being nobody and not becoming anything, but being able to just wait and to respond. And if there's nothing much to respond to, it's just waiting – coffee cup, watching the rain, the sunset, getting old, witnessing the ageing process, the comings and goings in the monastery – the ordinations and the disrobings, the inspirations and the depressions, the highs and the lows, inside the mind, outside in the world. And there is the response because when we have vigour and intelligence and talent, then life always comes to us asking us to respond to it in some skilful and compassionate way, which we are very willing and able to do. We like to help people. I wouldn't mind going to a Buddhist leper colony – I'd be glad to – or working in the shanty towns of Calcutta or wherever, I'd have no objections; those kinds of things are rather appealing to my sense of nobility!

But it's not a mission, it's not *me* having to do anything; it's trusting in the Dhamma. Then the response to life is clear and of benefit because it's not coming from me as a person and the delusions of ignorance conditioning mental formations. And one observes the restlessness, the compulsiveness, the obsessiveness of the mind and lets it cease. We let it go and it ceases.

NON-DUALISM

The significant offering of the Buddhist teaching lies in what we call non-dualism. Its the 'neither-nor' approach to philosophical questions. Monistic religion tends to talk about the One, the One God or the Whole or the Buddha Nature or the One Mind, and that's very inspiring. We turn to monistic doctrines for inspiration. But inspiration is only one level of religious experience, and you have to outgrow it. You have to let go of the desire for inspiration, or the belief in God or in the Oneness or in the One Mind or the all-embracing benevolence or in the universal fairness.

I am not asking you to disbelieve those things either. But the non-dualistic practice is a way of letting go of all that, of seeing attachment to the views and opinions and perceptions because the perception of one's mind is a perception, isn't it? The perception of a universal benevolence is a perception which we can attach to. The Buddha-Nature is a perception. Buddha is a perception. The One God and everything as being one universal system, global village, all is one and one is all and everything is fair and everything is kind, God loves us: these are perceptions which might be very nice, but still they are perceptions which arise and cease. Perceptions of monistic doctrines arise and cease.

Now what does that do, as a practical experience, when you let things go and they cease? What's left, what's the remainder? This is what the Buddha is pointing to in teaching about the arising and cessation of conditions.

When the perception of self ceases and all the doctrines, all the inspired teaching, all the wise sayings cease, there is still the knower of the cessation. And that leaves us with a blank mind. What is there to grasp? So the desire to know, to have something to grasp, comes up. We can see a panic in our minds sometimes: we've got to believe in something! 'Tell me about the universal benevolence!' But that's fear and desire operating again, isn't it? 'I want to believe in something! I need something to believe in! I want to know that everything is all right. I want to attach and believe in the perceptions of oneness and wholeness.' And so there is still that desire operating which you may not notice and may still be attached to. That's why the religious experience is one of despair.

In the story of the crucifixion, the most impressive statement Christ made was: 'Father, father why hast thou forsaken me?' What happened to that Father that was protecting Jesus? Even God left him. That's an anguished cry, isn't it? The one perception 'me' could count on suddenly dissolved in his mind. And after that, of course, is the acceptance and then the Resurrection, the being born anew to be free from all that illusion, from all that attachment to God, attachment to the doctrine and attachment to the highest ideas – the finest values.

All these things are still very good and praiseworthy. But it's through attachment that we suffer because if we attach to any perception, we are not realising the truth. We are just attaching to a symbol, and grasping the symbol to be the reality. If I said, 'You see the Buddha sitting up there on the shrine? That's the real Buddha. That is Buddha.' You'd think, 'Ajahn Sumedho has really gone off.' Yet we can still attach to a perception of Buddha as Buddha, can't we? We are not at the stage where we are going to believe that the vast statue is Buddha, but we can be very attached to a view about Buddha. And it might be a very nice view also. Just like that Buddha-rupa, it is a very nice Buddha-rupa, isn't it? I like that Buddha, it is very beautiful. It doesn't mean that we have to get rid of it, because Buddha-rupas do not delude. What is dangerous is our attachment to a perception – of self, of others, of Buddha, of God, of Oneness or of wholeness.

When you can actually free your mind from attachment then all these particular angles are valid. We are not condemning monism as a wrong. But attachment to monistic doctrine is limiting and blinding. Just like attachment to non-dualism. The purpose of non-dualism is really a tremendous pointing at attachment. But if you are just a philosophical non-dualist, then you can be attached to an attitude of annihilation.

I am not asking you to attach to a position of non-dualism but I have asked you not to try to inspire your mind or to read about inspired monistic teaching and various other religions during this retreat because in order to really learn how to use this particular tool, you have to use it and observe the results. And it can seem pretty barren. But we have to let go of that need for inspiration right up to the point of despair. We have to learn to accept that emptiness, that silence, the cessation, the loneliness, the lack of warmth, and not ask for benevolence and kindness. We have to open to the silence and contemplate it, learning from it rather than running away from it to look for a warm mother or a safe father.

Then one way you can describe this Holy Life is a growing up of an individual being to that maturity where we no longer linger in the warmth of adolescence or childhood, or in the pleasures of the world.

Dasadhammasutta

Bhikkhus, there are ten dhammas which should be reflected upon again and again by one who has gone forth. What are these ten ?

1) I am no longer living according to worldly aims and values.
   This should be reflected upon again and again by one who has gone forth.
2) My very life is sustained through the gifts of others.
   This should be reflected upon again and again by one who has gone forth.
3) I should strive to abandon my former habits
   This should be reflected upon again and again by one who has gone forth.
4) Does regret over my conduct arise in my mind?
   This should be reflected upon again and again by one who has gone forth.
5) Could my spiritual companions find fault with my conduct?
   This should be reflected upon again and again by one who has gone forth.
6) All that is mine, beloved and pleasing, will become otherwise, will become separated from me.
   This should be reflected upon again and again by one who has gone forth.
7) I am the owner of my kamma, heir to my kamma, born of my kamma, related to my kamma, abide supported by my kamma; whatever kamma I should do, for good or for ill, of that I will be the heir.
   This should be reflected upon again and again by one who has gone forth.
8) The days and nights are relentlessly passing, how well am I spending my time?

This should be reflected upon again and again by one who has gone forth.

9) Do I delight in solitude or not?

This should be reflected upon again and again by one who has gone forth.

10) Has my practice borne fruit with freedom or insight, so that at the end of my life, I need not feel ashamed when questioned by my spritual companions?

This should be reflected upon again and again by one who has gone forth.

Bhikkhus, these are the ten dhammas to be reflected upon again and again by one who has gone forth.

DEPENDENT ORIGINATION I: IGNORANCE IS THE SELF-VIEW

The uniqueness of the Buddhist approach is *anatta* – the realisation of not-self. The particular style of reflection in structures like the Four Noble Truths and the *paticcasamuppada* changes the way of thinking from the self-view – of the soul and 'me' as an absolute – to *anatta* – the not-self.

The problem lies in the fact that 'not-self' sounds like annihilation, doesn't it? And what frightens people about Buddhism is that 'not-self' and 'no soul' sounds like an absolute position that one has to take as a Buddhist. People that hate God and resent Christianity may become Buddhist because they've got a grudge against God, the soul, sin and guilt. They really want Buddhism to be a kind of atheistic philosophy and a total rejection of the whole Christian experience. But that's not what it is. Buddhism is not atheistic or nihilistic. The Buddha was very careful to avoid such extreme positions.

Instead, his teaching is a very skilfully and carefully constructed psychology. Its aim is to help us see through and let go of all the habitual attachments – attitudes born out of ignorance, fear and desire – that create this illusory sense of a self. So for 2530 years now Buddhism has managed to survive and keep its purity. And that is because its approach is very clear. There is a Sangha living under the Vinaya discipline, and there's the teaching of the Dhamma.

If we practise with this in the right way, we can really begin to see the suffering and misery we create over these illusions about ourselves. But we're not trying to create an illusion that there isn't any self. The point is not to go from the illusion of self to the illusion of 'there is no self.' but rather to investigate, contemplate and have the insight until the ineffable truth is realised, each one of us for oneself.

Each one of us has our unique experience – we are not experiencing exactly the same things. We have different memories, experiences, tendencies and habits. And yet we always relate these infinite varieties to Dhamma teachings so that we are not just making totally subjective interpretations. We apply the Dhamma teaching to our experience in order to be able to communicate and understand it in a context that is wider than that of personal subjectivity.

Often, people go off in practice when their religious experiences are interpreted too subjectively. They're not put across in a form that can be communicated. They become unique personal experiences rather than universal realisations. As was the case with Christian Gnosticism, you end up with all kinds of very strange subjective interpretations of mystical experience. Each gnostic had his own way of talking, so the Roman Catholic Church at the time said: 'This is madness!' and banned it all. But the Buddha established a whole way of thinking and expressing the teachings that is exactly the same today. We don't change and bend it all to fit our personal experience. We measure our experience with the teaching because the teachings are so skilfully made that they cover everything.

In contemplation of *paticcasamuppada*, we're coming to agreements on how its terms relate to contemplative experience. When you first read *paticcasamuppada*, you don't get it at all. 'Ignorance conditions kammic formations; kammic formations condition consciousness etc.' So what? What does that mean? You imagine it must be very profound and probably takes a lifetime of studying Pali to understand it. So you tend to brush it aside.

In Buddhist circles, the Four Noble Truths can be glossed over. 'Oh yes – basic Buddhism. Yes... now let's get on to the real advanced Madhyamika Buddhism!' Or, 'what did Dogen say?' Or, 'Milarepa is absolutely fascinating, isn't he?' And you think: ' "Suffering, Origin, Cessation and Path", yes, we know that, now let's get onto the real nitty-gritty.'

So the Four Noble Truths tend to be perfunctory beliefs. People don't investigate or use them because the teachings in themselves are not interesting, are they? 'Suffering, Origin, Cessation and Path' is not an inspiring teaching because it is a teaching for practice – not a teaching to inspire. And this is why we use it: because that particular way of thinking and contemplating is, psychologically, of great value.

With this we can begin to understand that which we've never seen or understood before. In following this way of practice, you're actually developing your mind and intelligence in a way that is very seldom done. Even in the most advanced educations, people don't really train their minds in this particular way of reflection and contemplation. To think rationally is highly regarded. But to understand what rationality *is* as a function of mind, you have to reflect on the nature of the mind. What is actually happening? What is it all about? And, of course, these are the questions of existence, aren't they? The existential questions: 'Why was I born?' 'Is there a meaning to life?' 'What happens when I die?' 'What is it all about?' 'Is it meaningless – just a cosmic accident?' 'Does it relate to anything beyond itself or is this merely something that happens and then that's it – that's the end?'

We have great problems with relating the meaning of life to anything real beyond just the material world. So materialism becomes the reality for us. When we explore space, it's always on the material plane. We want to go up in rocket ships and take our bodies up to the moon because according to the materialist view that's what's real. Western materialism lacks subtlety and refinement: it brings us down to a very coarse level of consciousness, where reality is this gross material object and the emotions are dismissed as not being real because they're subjective. You can't go round measuring emotions with electronic instruments.

But the emotions of course are *very* real to us individually – what we're feeling is more important to us than what's on a digital watch. Our fears and desires and loves and hates and aspirations are what really make our lives happy or miserable. And yet these can be dismissed in modern materialism for a world based on sensual pleasure, material wealth and rational thinking, so that the spiritual life to many people seems to be just an illusion. You can't measure it with a computer or examine it with electronic instruments.

Yet in pre-scientific European civilisation, the spiritual world was the real world. How do you think they built the cathedrals? And art – all this came from a real sense of spiritual aspiration, of the human being connected to something beyond the material world. Spiritual truth is something each one must realise individually. Truth is self-realisation, the ultimate subjectivity. And the Buddha takes subjectivity to the very centre of the universe, the silent still point, where the subject is not a *personal* subject. That still point is not anybody's or any thing.

In meditation, you're moving towards that. You're letting go of all these attachments to the changing conditions of the material world, the emotional plane, the intellectual plane, the symbolic plane and the astral plane. All that is let go of in order to realise the still point, the silence. This letting go is not an annihilation or a rejection, but it gives you the perspective to understand the whole. You cannot understand the whole from being out on the circumference where you just get whirled around.

Being whirled around on the circumference means that you're lost in attachment to all the things that are whirling around. It's called *samsara*, where you're just going around in circles. You can't get any perspective in *samsara*. You have no ability to stop and watch or observe because you're just caught in this circular movement.

The aim of meditation in this way of the Four Noble Truths and *paticcasamuppada* is to stop the mind's whirling. You actually abide in the stillness, not as an attack against the conditioned world but in order to see it in perspective. You're not annihilating it or criticising it or trying to get out of it in any way through aversion or fear of it. But you're getting to the centre, to the still point where you can see it for what it is and know it and not be frightened or deluded by it anymore. And we do this within the limitation of our personal experience. So we can say: 'Each one for themselves.' because that's how it looks when we're sitting here. And yet that still point is not in the mind, it's not in the body. This is where it's ineffable. The full mind or the still point isn't a point within the brain. Yet you're realising that universal silence, stillness, oneness where all the rest is a reflection and seen in perspective. And the personality, the kamma, the differences, the varieties and all these things are no longer deluding us because we're no longer grasping at them.

As we examine the mind more and more, as we reflect and contemplate on it and learn from it, we all begin to realise the stillness of mind, which is always present but which, with most people, is not even noticed. This is because the life of *samsara* is so busy, so frantic, that one is whirled around. Even though the still point is always here, it's never seen until you take the occasion to abide in the stillness rather than go around on the circumference.

Not that stillness is something to attach to either! We're not trying to become people who are still – just sitting here in stillness, not feeling anything. I know that some of you come in here and create a personal world that you can inhabit through the hour of meditation. But that's not the way out of suffering; that subjective and personal world is very dependent on things being a certain way. It is so fragile and so ephemeral that it is destroyed with the slightest disruption. The refined world of tranquillity is so lovely, so peaceful – then somebody moves their robes. Somebody's stomach growls, somebody snores! It's disgusting, isn't it, to be disrupted out of these fine tranquil states by coarse bodily functions.

But stillness isn't tranquillity. It's not necessary that we're tranquil, but there's stillness when we can trust in abiding in the silence rather than following our compulsive tendencies. We all tend to think we've got to be doing something; we're so conditioned to do things that even meditation becomes a compulsive activity that we're involved in. 'Develop this . . . develop that. . . . I have to develop my *samadhi*, and I have to develop the *jhanas*.' You don't just come in here and sit, you come in here and *develop*! That's how we think! We feel guilty if we are not doing anything, progressing, developing, getting anywhere. And yet to be able to come in here and sit in stillness is not a very easy thing to do is it? It's much easier to make great meditation development projects, five-year plans and so forth. Yet you always end up at the still point: things as they are.

With understanding more and more, there can be a letting go of the desire to develop and become anything. And as one's mind is freed from all that desire to become and get something, to attain something, then Truth starts revealing itself. It's ever-present, here and now. It's a matter of just being able to be open and sensitive so that Truth is revealed. It's not something that is revealed from outside. The Truth is always present but we don't see it if we're caught up in the idea of attainments, of 'me' having to do something, of 'me' having to get something.

So the Buddha made this direct attack on 'me and mine'. That's the only thing that's blocking you up. The obstacle is the attachment to a self-view. If you just see through that self-view, let go of that, then you'll understand the rest. You don't need to know all the other elaborate esoteric formulas or anything. You don't have to go endlessly on into the complexity if you just let go of the ignorant view of 'I am.'

See that, and know and understand the way of letting go, of non-attachment. Then the Truth reveals itself wherever you are, all the time. But until you do that then you'll always be caught in creating problems and complications.

'*Avijjapaccaya sankhara; sankharapaccaya viññanam; viññanapa-caya namarupam; namarupapaccaya salayatanam; salayatanapaccaya phasso; phassapaccaya vedana; vedanapaccaya tanha; tanhapaccaya upadanam; upadanapaccaya bhavo; bhavapaccaya jati; jatipaccaya jaramaranam-soka-parideva-dukkha-domanassupayasa.*'*

All this means if you keep insisting on being attached to the illusions of a self, to greed, hatred and delusion, all you're going to ever get at the end is old age, sickness and death, grief, sorrow, despair and anguish. That's all you'll get for the rest of your life: pretty boring prospect, isn't it!

But you can be free from that here and now, through this Right Understanding, seeing things in the right way. There can be the knowing of Truth in which one is no longer deluded by appearances or habits, or by the conditions around us.

---

* This is the formulation, in the Pali language of the scriptures, of the teaching on Dependent Origination (*paticcasamuppada*). The translation of this is in the Introduction; the main thrust of its message is contained in the English that follows it.

DEPENDENT ORIGINATION II:
MOMENTARY ARISING

In Ajahn Buddhadasa's book on Dependent Origination, he emphasises that his approach has been on the *paticcasamuppada* as working in the moment rather than in terms of past, present and future lives. When you contemplate, when you practise, you realise that that is the only way it could ever be. This is because we are working with the mind itself. Even when we are considering the birth of a human body, we are not commenting on the birth of our own bodies, but recognising mentally that these bodies were born. Then, in reflection, we are noting that mental consciousness arises and ceases. So that whole sequence of Dependent Origination arises and ceases in a moment. The arising and the cessation from *avijja* is momentary, it is not a kind of permanent *avijja*. It would be a mistaken view to assume that everything began with *avijja* and sometime in the future it would all cease.

Avijja means in this sense 'not understanding the Four Noble Truths.' When there is understanding of Suffering, Origin, Cessation and Path, then things are no longer affected by *avijja*. When we see with *vijja*, then the perceptions are conventional reality, no longer 'me' and 'mine.' For example, when there is *vijja*, then I can say 'I am Ajahn Sumedho' – that is a conventional reality, still a perception but it is no longer viewed from *avijja*, it's merely a convention we use. There's nothing more to it than that. It is as it is.

When we get to cessation of ignorance, then at that moment, all the rest of the sequence ceases. It is not like one ceases, *then* another ceases. When there is *vijja*, then the suffering ceases. In any moment, when there is true mindfulness and wisdom, there is no suffering. The suffering has ceased. Now when you contemplate the cessation of desire, cessation of grasping, there is the cessation of becoming, cessation of rebirth and suffering. When things cease, when everything ceases, then there's peace, isn't there? There is knowing, serenity, emptiness, not-self. These are the words, the concepts describing cessation.

When I practise in this way, it is very difficult to find any suffering. I realise there isn't any suffering except in a heedless moment when one gets carried away with something. So because of heedlessness and lack of attention and forgetting , we get caught in habitual (kammic) mind stuff. But when we realise we have been heedless, we can let it cease, we can let go. There is the letting go, the abiding in emptiness. No longer are there the strong impulses to grasp; the fascination and the glamour of the sensory world has been penetrated. No longer is there anything to grasp. One can still experience and see the way things are without grasping it. There's nobody grasping anything, but there can still be feeling and seeing and hearing, taste and touch. It is no longer created into a person . . . 'me and mine'.

For me, the important insight is just how momentary consciousness is. The tendency is to perceive consciousness as a long-term thing, as being awake and being conscious as a permanent state of being rather than a moment. And yet, *viññana* is always described as a moment, a flashing moment, an instant. So rather than assume that *avijja* is a continuous process from the birth out of our bodies, we can see that at any moment there can be *vijja* and the whole thing just ceases. The cessation of that whole mass of suffering can be realised. It's gone! Where is it?

To practise this way is to keep examining things so that everything is seen exactly for what it is. Everything is only what it is in the moment. When we see that, beauty is just beauty in the moment. Ugliness is just that in the moment. There is no attempt to solidify that or prolong that in any way because things are just what they are. One is increasingly aware of the formless or nebulous as just what it is rather than as something that is overlooked, dismissed or misinterpreted.

The problem of perception is that it tends to limit us to just being conscious of certain points. We tend to be conscious in certain designated points and the natural change and flux and flow is not really noticed. One is only conscious at the A, B, C, D, E, F, G – the points between A and B are never really noticed because one is only really conscious at the designated points of perception. That is why when the mind is opened with *vijja* and is receptive, then Dhamma reveals itself, there is a kind of revelation. The empty mind in the state of wonder allows truth to be revealed – not through perception anymore. This is where it is ineffable truth, words fail us and it is impossible to put it into perceptions or concepts.

Maybe now you are beginning to appreciate the emphasis the Buddha made: 'I teach suffering and the end of suffering. I teach only two things . . . there is suffering and there is the end of suffering.' If you have just that insight into understanding suffering and realise the end of suffering, then you are liberated from ignorance. If you attempt to speculate on what that is like, you could call it 'Nibbana, the highest happiness' – but 'highest happiness' is not quite it either, is it? 'Highest happiness' sounds like getting high, floating in the air, reaching Nibbana and floating up to the ceiling.

But the Way is one of realisation; mindfulness and realisation. Then the eightfold path is development, *bhavana*: to develop that path to right understanding. More and more we realise the emptiness, the not-self, the freedom from not being attached to anything; which affects what we say, what we do and how we live in the society we are in by increasing the sense of serenity and calm.

That word Nibbana is generally defined as 'non-attachment to the five *khandhas*,' which means no longer experiencing a sense of a self in regard to the body and mind – *rupa*, *vedana*, *sañña*, *sankhara*, *viññana*. We contemplate the five *khandhas* not with *avijja* anymore but with *vijja*. We see that they are all impermanent, unsatisfactory and not-self. Then Nibbana is the realisation of non-attachment wherein the self-view ceases. The body is still breathing, so it doesn't dissolve into thin air, but the mistaken identity that 'I am the body' dissolves. The mistaken identity with *vedana, sañña, sankhara* and *viññana* – all that ceases. The self dissolves, you can't find anybody. You can't find yourself because you *are* yourself.

In the view of Dependent Origination occurring over the span of three lives, the five *khandhas* are seen as a permanent form from birth. The body: feelings, perceptions, mind formations and consciousness, are considered as being continuous from birth. But that's an assumption we make — and the reflection of momentary arising points to the mind itself. The body isn't a person anyway, it's not 'me' and 'mine', never was, never will be. There's only the *perception* of it as 'me' and 'mine'. The *belief* that I was born.

I've a birth certificate to prove that this body was born. We carry birth certificates in our minds – we carry around the whole history, the memories and so forth of our lives, giving us this sense of the continuity of a person from birth to the present moment. But examination of perception alone shows that perception arises and ceases. This perception of me as a permanent personality is just a moment. It arises and ceases. Consciousness, too, is just momentary and conveys the attractive, repulsive and neutral qualities of the conditioned realm. When one sees that clearly, then there is no interest anymore in that attachment and in seeking for happiness, trying to be reborn into happiness or beauty, pleasure, safety or security. Rebirth is a grasping of the conditioned realm so we let that go. The five *khandhas* are still the five *khandhas;* they are seen for what they are as impermanent, unsatisfactory and not-self.

So this reflection on the truth of the way it is – it's very direct, very clear. From the confused, amorphous, nebulous, insecure, unstable, uncertain to the certain – whatever it is, we are no longer choosing which we prefer, we are just noting that whatever arises ceases. As you realise this through your practice, then a lot of the vagueness, and fuzziness of your mind are seen for exactly what they are. Confusion is confusion, just that, it's a *dhamma*. Confusion is just confusion in the moment, it's not permanent or the self. So what before was a problem or something deluding us is transformed into a *dhamma*. The transformation is not through changing the condition but through changing the attitude, from ignorance to clarity.

People say: 'All this is very well but what about love and compassion?' The *desire* for all that is the block, isn't it? Love is no problem once there is no delusion, once there is no self, there's nothing to hinder or block off or prevent love. But as long as there is self-illusion then love is just an idea that we long for but are always feeling disappointed with because the self is getting in the way. The self-view is always blinding us, making us forget and imagine that there isn't any love. We feel alienated and lonely and lost because there doesn't seem to be any love, so we blame somebody else, or we blame ourselves, maybe because we're not loveable, or we become cynics.

But the Buddha pointed to this and asked what was the real problem? It's the illusion of a self. It's the attachment to that perception. That affects the consciousness so we are always creating the separations and the dissatisfaction, and identifying with that which is not ourselves. Once we are free from that illusion, then love is ever-present. It's just that we can't see it or enjoy it when we are blinded by our desires and fears.

As you understand this more and more, your faith increases and there is a willingness to give up everything. There is a real zest, a joy in being with the way things are.

DEPENDENT ORIGINATION III:
THE FORMATIONS OF SELF

A*vijjapaccaya sankhara:* this means: 'ignorance conditions the kammic formation', i.e. body and mind as defined by the five *khandhas.* That is when we operate from a position of ignorance, not understanding the truth, and everything that we experience and do and say and feel is conditioned from that ignorance. Absolutely everything.

This is where the self-view is such a blind spot. When we think of the kammic formation as 'self' rather than as 'not-self' then everything that happens, everything that is experienced, is referred to that sense of a person – 'me' as a perception. This is *avijjapaccaya sankhara.*

If you have the insight that all conditions are impermanent, all dhamma is not-self, then there's knowing or *vijja,* and truth or Dhamma rather than ignorance (*avijja*) and habitual kamma (*sankhara*). There's knowing the Dhamma, the truth of the way it is. Then all the rest follows suit, everything is seen as it is. There's no distortion: consciousness and the five aggregates and the sense world are seen as Dhamma rather than as self.

What is your suffering in life, anyway? Why do you suffer? If you investigate, you can always trace it back to *avijjapaccaya sankhara.* There's natural suffering, going hungry, getting old and getting sick, but that's all bearable. That's nothing that we can't bear. Sickness, old age and death is something we can always bear with. That's not real suffering. But the suffering is the greed, hatred and delusion we produce through the self-view, through taking it all personally. The creations and attachments to wrong views and prejudices and biases and all the horrors that we are responsible for can all be traced back to *avijjapaccaya sankhara.*

We can't really expect very much improvement if we still insist on being ignorant, caught in the self-view. Even though we might be able to improve conditions slightly by trying to be a good person, as long as there is attachment to self-view, there is delusion; so even the goodness we do comes from delusion. It doesn't lead anyone out of suffering. If we don't have wisdom, then often we try to do good but we end up causing all kinds of problems, while thinking we can tell others what is good for them.

What is the way it is at this moment? Your body is sitting, isn't it? You can feel things – pleasure, pain, heat or cold or whatever. This is the way things are. There's no self in that; we are not creating the self. When we bring our attention to the way things are, we can see what we do when we create the 'me' and 'mine' onto the moment: what I think, what I feel, what I want, what I don't want, what I like, what I don't like, or we can be aware of the selves we create in others: my opinions about you. I have suffered a lot from creating people in my mind, not because anybody was really cruel to me, but because of all the things I used to make out about myself and about other people – the fear of what others thought; the jealousies, the envy, the greed, the possessiveness. I would have my prejudices and views about people, what I think they are really up to, and my suspicions about what they really want. So that suffering comes out of the creation we make about ourselves and others, about our parents, and about the people closest to us.

What is suffering? Really ask yourself, what is the suffering of your life? Yesterday the cold winds were blowing through me as I was walking out there in the field. Is that suffering? I could make it suffering. 'I hate this cold wind and I don't like it.' But actually it was all right. I mean, it was something I could completely bear. If I didn't make anything about it in my mind, it was just cold wind – that's all.

Yet we can spend time in Amaravati creating attitudes about monks, nuns, lay people. You can really make senior nuns into big ogres, can't you? We can have strong views about seniority. If we are in a senior position we can be very attached to it. 'I am senior to you. You are just a new monk. Do that. I'm boss.' So we can create ourselves as being senior monks. But we are not here to create *kamma* based on ignorance. The conventions we have are merely expedient means. They are simplifications, moral agreements and community agreements, to make life simple and uncomplicated and also to allow us to reflect on the way we relate to people; people senior, people the same, people junior.

The Buddha said*: 'The view that everybody is equal is a delusion.' 'I am superior to everyone' is a delusion. 'I am inferior' is a delusion. 'I am' is a delusion, if that identity is based on ignorance. But when there's *vijja*, then 'I am' is merely conventional reality. It's just the way we talk: 'I am hungry,' or 'I am Sumedho Bhikkhu' – but it's not a person.

When there's *avijja*, that conditions the *sankhara* which conditions the consciousness or *viññana*. Consciousness conditions mentality and corporeality(*nama-rupa*), which conditions the sense bases (*salayatana*), which conditions contact (*phassa*), which conditions feeling (*vedana*). When ignorance is the primary condition, the rest are all affected by that. The sensory world, the body and mind, are related to in terms of 'me' and 'mine'. This is the self-view. Now in contrast to Brahmanism where the Hindu talks about the Atman or the 'higher self', the One, when the Buddha talks of self, it is related to attachment to the five *khandhas*, to body, feeling, perceptions, volitions and consciousness; the attachment to that, the ignorance, conditions kammic formations. All this creates a sense of a self.

This self-view starts getting strong when you are around six to seven years old. You go to school and you compete and you compare, and this strong sense of a self starts being conditioned into your mind. I remember the first five or six years of my life being magical, and then after six or seven, it started getting increasingly worse. Before that, there wasn't very much sense of self.

In a country like the States – which is a very nice country, actually – there is an emphasis on self-view. There is not a tremendous amount of wisdom in that country and the personality view is very much the dominant theme. 'I am an individual, I have my rights.

---

*For example Sutta-Nipata 860: 'Having finished with envy and greed, the sage does not speak of 'superior', 'inferior', or 'equal'.

I can do what I want. You can't tell me what to do. Who do you think you are? I'm as good as you are. Get off my back.' The egalitarian Americans have their strong attachments to being an individual with a fascinating personality, a real character, a 'good guy.' This is the American emphasis on the personal level. Being a 'good guy' is all right; there's nothing wrong with it, but as *avijjapaccaya sankhara* it can only bring suffering. When there is ignorance and self-view, the 'good guy' is always going to suffer.

Avijja conditions the *sankhara*, which conditions consciousness, which conditions mentality-corporeality, which conditions the six senses, which conditions contact and then feeling, and then feeling conditions desire – the *vedana-tanha* connection. You can notice that if you are caught in attachment to personality view or self, then there is going to be desire, grasping (*upadana*) and becoming (*bhava*). You will be lost in that pattern because when there is ignorance in *this* moment, that affects everything – consciousness, senses and the sense-objects, the feeling and then the desire comes into it. 'I want something.' 'I want to be happy.' 'I want to become.' 'I want to get rid of' – the 'I want.'

Examine desire during this retreat, really get to know what desire is. From my own reflection on it, I see it is always energy aiming at something, whether it's restless and scattered or aimed at something definite. There is a strong desire to get rid of things we don't like as quickly as possible. We want to get what we want instantly and get rid of what we don't like instantly; we don't value patience any more in our society. We want efficiency. Everything looks nice and then something comes in and makes a mess and we have to clean it up immediately because we don't want obstacles or hindrances or anything unpleasant. We want to get rid of it quickly, so we are very impatient and we can get very upset and annoyed at things because of this desire to get rid of, this *vibhava -tanha*.

The desire to become, ambition, *bhava-tanha* is often a motivation within the religious life – we want to become an enlightened personality. So *bhava-tanha* and *vibhava-tanha* are to be studied and examined.

You can reflect on them; you can listen to these desires: 'I want to get enlightened.' 'I want to get samadhi. I want to make the best I can out of this retreat so I can have some kind of achievement or attainment from it all.' We also want to get rid of things: 'I hope I get rid of all my lust and anger during this retreat. I hope to get rid of the jealousy so I never have to be jealous again. During this retreat I am working on jealousy. I'm working on doubt or fear – if I can get rid of my fear by the end of this retreat, I will have no more fear left because I'm going to get right in there and annihilate fear.' That's *vibhava-tanha*! 'There is something wrong with me and I have got to make it right. I have to become something else by getting rid of these bad things, these wrong things about me.' It's all the 'I am's' and the 'me-and-mine.'

Kama-tanha is quite obvious – it is the desire for pleasurable sense experiences. These forms of desire are to be known and *understood*. The trap is that we tend to think that the Buddha teaches you to get rid of your desires. That is how some people interpret Buddhism. But that's wrong: the Buddha taught us how to *look* and *understand* desire so that we do not grasp it! That's not telling us to get rid of desire but to really understand it so that desire can no longer delude us. The desire to get rid of desire is still desire, it is not looking at desire. With that desire, you are just grasping a perception that you shouldn't have desires and you have to get rid of them. But understanding Dependent Origination, we see the *tanha* as Dhamma rather than as self – you are looking at *tanha*, the desire as that which arises and ceases. That's Dhamma, isn't it? In twenty-five years of careful looking and close observation I have not found one desire that arises and keeps arising. If any of you do find one, please tell me.

Kama-tanha is fairly coarse and fairly obvious – I want something to eat – or sexual desires. But *vibhava-tanha* can be very subtle and righteous and important. And one can be deluded by that righteous quality. The desire to get rid of evil can seem so right. We can really dedicate our lives to getting rid of the evils in this world and become fanatical. This is what you can see in modern social problems. There are the degenerate tendencies of this society that go into sexual aberrations and drugs and then there are the very righteous forms of fundamentalists that condemn the degenerate, loose-living, immoral behaviour of one element of society. But we are looking at desire itself, from the gross forms of want and lust to righteous passion of 'wanting to kill and annihilate these degenerates!'

Contemplate that as something within your mind. I have seen both tendencies in myself. I can become attracted to sensual pleasures. And I can also be really hard and self-righteous, and critical of others or of myself. *Bhava-tanha* can be very sweet too when you are doing it for the welfare of others. It's not just that I want to attain something so I can say that I have attained something. There is also the *bhava-tanha* of wanting because you feel you would like to help everyone else. There is still the 'I am.' 'I want to get enlightened and then I am going to really help everyone else and I want to become someone who is not selfish but works totally for the welfare of all sentient beings.' That's very altruistic, isn't it? It's beautiful and it is inspiring, but it can also be *bhava-tanha* if it is coming from *avijja-pacaya sankhara*.

When we see clearly with *vijja* and see Dhamma, then there is nobody to become anything or to achieve or to attain. Things are as they are. Good is done and bad is refrained from in action and speech. There is doing good. What is there left to do in life but to be virtuous? Isn't that the beauty of our humanity? What is truly joyful and lovely about being human is our ability to be virtuous. I can't think of anything else to do. The human experience is for virtue and goodness and refraining from doing evil harmful things to ourselves and others. I can't think of anything else worth doing!

DEPENDENT ORIGINATION IV:
FEELING CONDITIONS DESIRE

In the beginning of the practice of *paticcasamuppada* is *avijjapaccaya sankhara*: ignorance conditions the kammic formations. *Avijja* is the ignorance of not knowing the Four Noble Truths. There is ignorance in any being who does not understand that there is suffering, the arising of suffering, the cessation of suffering, and the Path leading to its cessation. Conversely, the word for knowledge in this sense is *vijja*. *Vijja* is the knowing of the four Noble Truths: the insight into suffering, origin, cessation and Path.

When we haven't had insight into Truth, *avijja*, not knowing, conditions the *sankhara*. We create an 'I am.' The *sankhara* 'I am' is created and conditioned from that *avijja*. If you notice, the First Noble Truth does not say 'I suffer'; the First Noble Truth says, 'There is suffering; there is *dukkha*.' It's not saying that anybody suffers. However, we think we suffer, don't we? We think, 'I suffer a lot in this life. . . . He's a real sufferer. . . . She suffers all the time. . . . I've suffered a lot in my life. I wasn't born with the best kammic formations available on this planet and I've really had to suffer. Poor me!' But the suffering is what we create out of ignorance. And so the important point the Buddha made was that we should live in accordance with knowledge rather than ignorance.

This Buddhist practice is a way of knowledge, of knowing; it's all about knowing the truth. That's why I don't particularly feel sorry for anybody when they think they suffer a lot. I could say, 'Poor thing. I really feel sorry for you that you've had to suffer.' But this thinking you are suffering is not the position of knowing. Things have happened in the past, perhaps unfortunate occurrences, and then we think and indulge – which carries it on in the present with all kinds of additional suffering. But when there's knowledge, insight, *vijja*, then we realise there's nobody to suffer. We see things as they are.

Every human being has the ability to see clearly the way things are and not create suffering about it.

Now admittedly, we've all experienced unfortunate things or done foolish things. This is just ordinary human experience, isn't it? When we're born, anything can happen to us. The whole range of life's experiences from the most fortunate to the most unfortunate ones are all possible for us. That's the result of birth. There's nothing wrong with that; it's just the way it is. Birth in the human realm is risky – we can't be sure what we're getting into. It could be a real mess or it could be a delight; it could also be sometimes messy and sometimes delightful or one-quarter messy, three-fourths mediocre and no delightful things at all.

Being born in this human world into sensory consciousness is like this: it's unstable, uncertain, it changes, and we cannot find any security within it. This is what we all have in common. From the most fortunate to the least fortunate human beings, we are all vulnerable, being in a shape and form that can be damaged, hurt and diseased. When we look at this side of our human existence, then we don't feel the prejudices and strong views of race and class and sex and nationality and so forth. We're all brothers and sisters in old age, sickness and death.

Having been born, there's *viññana*, consciousness, there's body, *nama-rupa*. There are sense organs – *salayatana* – the eye, ear, nose, tongue, body, mind. There is *phassa* or contact with the sense objects; and there's *vedana*, feeling. This *vedana* is the result of birth and consciousness, and, in this sense, is applied to sensory experience, to the attractive, neutral and unattractive qualities. The experience of *vedana* through the eyes doesn't mean your eyes ache or hurt; it means that when you see beautiful flowers as attractive that the *vedana* of attraction is pleasant. There is also unpleasant or neutral feeling. Then that whole process will stimulate desire, grasping and becoming (*tanha-upadana-bhava*). We become what we desire. Now apply that to all the senses and their objects – to sound, smell, taste, touch and thought. Some of our thoughts are very pleasant; some are neither pleasant nor unpleasant, and some are unpleasant.

This is the sensitivity of these bodies; they're totally sensitive conditions; they're conscious and they feel. This is just the way it is. Some of you only want to be partially sensitive, don't you? You're frightened of being totally sensitive. You'd like to become only sensitive to nice things, and you'd like to pray to God and say: 'Oh

God, please give me everything nice, only pleasant feelings, and please make everything beautiful for me. Never let me suffer, and let me always have success and happiness and beautiful people around me until I die. . . .' And that's the whinging human mind wanting only partial sensitivity.

The *vijja* or the insight knowledge is knowing the pleasant and neutral and unpleasant as they are. We're not asking for partial sensitivity any more or for the best of the sensory experiences, but we are opening towards total sensitivity which includes all possibilities for pain, ugliness, unpleasantness. *Avijja* says: 'I don't want to lose my looks; I don't want to have any unpleasant experiences; I want to be happy.' That's *avijja*. *Vijja* says: 'There is suffering; there is the origin and the cessation, and there is the way out of suffering.'

So contemplate this 'I am' during this retreat, this 'I am' that cries and weeps and fears and desires. Why are we frightened? What are we frightened of and anxious about? It is the possibility of pain, isn't it? Of being physically harmed, diseased, emotionally exploited or hurt in some way; being rejected, being unloved, being looked down on, getting cancer or Parkinson's disease. . . . 'I don't want that; I want perfect health. . . . I'm afraid I might have some terrible disease.   What if I have one of those heart attacks where for the next thirty to forty years I'm a kind of cabbage and the monks have to do everything, put me on the potty. . . .? I don't want that, I couldn't bear to be a nuisance or a burden to anyone.' 'I don't want to be a burden'   that's an English obsession, isn't it?

So the 'I am' is something to contemplate and observe because this is something that we're convinced is reality for us. For most human beings, 'I am' is truth because of ignorance. And then it's very natural to want happiness and want to run away from pain. You see something beautiful, you grasp it, you want it. Something ugly – you want to get rid of it. That's the natural reaction on the sensory plane. If that's all there is to it, then you just have to try to get all the best you can and run away from all the bad, and there's no way out of it. It's each one for themselves – survival. The clever and the strong survive, and the stupid and the weak will be at the bottom, in the pits.

But the human being is equipped with a reflective mind; we can reflect and contemplate *vedana*. We can observe and contemplate what attraction is and what beauty is. We're not just dumb animals: we can actually watch ourselves wanting to grab and possess the beautiful. We can observe and reflect on our aversion to anything ugly and unpleasant; and we can also contemplate what is neither pleasant nor unpleasant.

Our normal breathing is neither pleasant nor unpleasant; it's neither attractive nor unattractive. So that's why you have to pay attention to it because if the breath were attractive it would attract you. I wouldn't have to say, 'Watch your breath' – you'd be watching your breath because it was so attractive!

Breathing is the most important physiological function, and the body does it whether we're aware of it, whether we're crazy or sane, young or old, male or female, rich or poor, or whatever. Breathing is this way. It's neither exciting nor interesting, nor is it disgusting or revolting. But as we concentrate, bring our attention to breathing of the body – what happens? Well, when I concentrate on my breath, the mind goes tranquil; I feel tranquillised by being able to concentrate on the breathing of this body.

Anapanasati is boring to most people at first; just inhalation-exhalation, the same old thing. The breathing of the body is neutral *vedana*. When we do the meditation of sweeping through the feeling of the body, the pressure of the body sitting on the seats and the clothes touching the skin: that's neutral feeling. Then we can observe the *vedana* through the ear, the nose, the tongue, the eye, the body, the mind. And we start to see that's just the sensory realm, that's not a person, that's just the way it is. There's nothing wrong with that, nothing bad about it at all. *Vedana* is all right. There's just the pleasant and the painful and the neutral; they're just what they are.

However, to be aware of pleasure and pain and of neutral *vedana* means that we have to bear it, to really accept it rather than just react to it. We reflect on it and contemplate it so that we really understand it. Now if we don't contemplate and have insight into *vedana*, we just continue this process of *paticcasamuppada* – so we have desires, because *vedana* conditions *tanha*: desire. But with insight, we can actually break the habit. We can contemplate *vedana*. Then we begin to understand how desire arises: wanting the pleasure, not wanting the pain, and just ignoring the neutral.

A person that lives a very fast life goes from one exciting, thrilling thing to the next. When we think of really exciting lifestyles, what does it usually involve? It is usually full of frantic attempts to have fantastic sensual experience; to be always running about – because yesterday's fantastic sensual experience is boring. There's a need to have new sensual experiences, new romances and adventures, because anything gets boring when it's repeated. So *samsara* is the cycle, the endless running about looking for the next interesting thing, the next excitement, the next romance, the next adventure – the next, the next, the next . . . notice how insidious that is in our lives. Even in the monastic life, even in a meditation retreat, we can still be caught up in trying to get onto the next thing; sitting here thinking about what we'll do after the retreat, or trying to find something to make our lives more interesting here at Amaravati.

What is interest? Things that are interesting are things that are attractive and hold our attention. We *want* to be attracted by something. We want attractive things, pleasurable experiences, beautiful objects, beautiful music and sounds. They are interesting, they hold our attention, they please and fascinate us. And if an experience is unpleasant, we dread it. It can be a hell-realm for most people, the idea of having to be in some place where there's nothing beautiful: dreary, boring people; gross and coarse and bad odours; men and women who have no culture; disgusting, foul, stinking evil brutes; pain, sickness. . . . That's what we dread, what we might end up with. It might happen that we get stuck in some miserable place. So we want to avoid and get rid of all of that and then try to get hold of the pleasant experiences as much as possible.

And yet most of our lives are neither pleasant nor painful *vedana*. When you contemplate most of your life, I'm sure that, for most of you, about 98% of your life has been neither pleasant nor painful. When I think of my life, about 2% has been highly pleasant and highly painful, and about 98% has been neither pleasant nor painful but just what it is. And yet that 98% of one's life can go by totally unnoticed because we are so attached to the extremes of waiting for the next thing, longing and expecting and hoping, and then dreading and fearing those possibilities of not having any more pleasure, not having a good time. Well, just think of our day here at Amaravati or anywhere in the world. How much of it is really pleasurable or painful?

The Buddha advised us to bring our attention to the neither-pleasant-nor-painful things in life because to accept and notice neither-pleasure-nor-pain means we have to be attentive and alert. If it's not attractive or repulsive, it doesn't make us react. It doesn't stimulate our minds at all. So we have to bring our attention to it, be awake to it. That's why, in meditation, we sit, we stand, we walk, we lie down; four basic postures, normal breathing, things that are so ordinary but are not pleasurable nor painful. The practice of mindfulness is to bring our attention to *vedana*. But we're not attaching to neutrality either: we're not trying to attach to neither pleasure nor pain. So to study *vedana*, we're not trying to live a neutral existence. But bringing attention to it means that we have to put effort to just sitting, standing, walking, lying down; being awake, being here and now. We have to pay attention, we have to learn to concentrate the mind.

Vedana conditions *tanha*. So what is *tanha*? This word is translated as desire. It's when you're not aware and alert to the way things are – then you want or do not want.

Starting from the *vedana*, if it's pleasurable you want it, if it's painful you don't want it. Then there's a sensual desire – *kama-tanha*, wanting sensory pleasures, just going around eating and drinking, listening to music and living a very distracted life of sensual delight. We all know that, don't we? Also, we've all experienced *bhava-tanha*, desire to become – ambition. 'I want to become something. I want to become a success; I want to become enlightened; I want to become good. I want to become admired and respected.' And *vibhava-tanha*: desire to get rid of – that's a strong one, too. 'Let's get rid of all the unpleasant things, the bad thoughts, the bad feelings, the pain, the imperfections' – the desire to get rid of.

We can observe these three kinds of desires: we can observe and reflect on them because they're objects of the mind; they're mind objects, they're not the subject. Desire is not you, in other words. But it becomes a subject; it becomes you out of heedlessness, out of *avijja*. You grasp desire and you *become* the desired . . . 'I want this and I don't want that. I want to become a success, I don't want to become a failure. I've got to get rid of these faults.' So there's the grasping of desire, and then you become somebody who wants things or doesn't want things. And that's endless, isn't it? When we *become* a person who wants things and doesn't want things, then it just goes on and on and on. There's always something we want and something we don't want. If we don't watch and observe this process, then our whole life is just this cycle, this endless cycle of *samsara* going around and around, just wanting; becoming somebody who wants something, becoming somebody who doesn't want something. And then that, of course, conditions rebirth, *jati*. It conditions old age, sickness, death, sorrow, lamentation, pain, grief and despair – depression, misery; *'jara-maranam -soka- parideva- dukkha- domanassa upayasa.'*

To be somebody who always has to get something or get rid of something is such a painful way to live. Just contemplate: what is the real suffering in your life? When you think you've suffered, what is it that you suffered from? It's from being somebody who wants things or doesn't want things. We talk about the First Noble Truth, *dukkha*. We all have this suffering. When there's *avijja* then we suffer, our life is going to be a realm of suffering.

This is becoming very obvious in affluent Western Europe, in places like America and Australia, affluent societies where people get very much what they want and where suffering isn't the suffering of starvation, deprivation and brutality. But there's so much misery and suffering in affluent countries. From what? Wanting and not wanting: because even when we get everything we want, there's more that we want and there are things that we don't want.

Just trying to satisfy all our desires and get everything we want is not the answer, is it? That's not the way out of suffering because that process doesn't end until you see it, until you use *vijja* rather than *avijja*. So contemplate that, this wanting and not wanting; desire and the grasping of desire.

When you contemplate *vedana*, then you see that's just a natural way: the attraction and repulsion and neither attractive nor repulsive. It's just being sensitive. For example, these flowers in front of me are attractive to me right now. That's just the natural way of things. There's no desire in that. If I just contemplate at this moment: 'I don't want those flowers,' there's no desire; I don't want to get rid of them. There's no wanting or not wanting, but they're still pleasing; their attractiveness is this way. That's the *vedana*. Another example is something ugly, like these curtains. I find them ugly. Whenever I come into this room my mind says, 'Those curtains are ugly.' So one doesn't really want to look at them. Now I can be aware of the displeasure when my eyes contact those curtains without desiring to get rid of them; it's just awareness of their unattractiveness – or when I see the wall, which is neither attractive nor unattractive, just a neutral wall.

Now reflecting this way, you see that's just the natural way of things: attraction and aversion, neither attractive nor averse, just the *vedana*. Then the desire is what we add, like for those flowers: 'Oh,

I really want those flowers, I want to have those flowers in my room, I've got to have those flowers!' Also the curtains: 'I wish they could get rid of those curtains – they really upset me!' One dwells on wanting to get rid of the curtains, wanting to grab the flowers, and of course, one doesn't even notice the wall unless something attractive or unattractive appears on it. And what about the space in the room? Space is neither attractive nor unattractive, is it?

So contemplate in this way. What is desire? When you're feeling pain in your body, if you reflect on the actual physical sensation of pain, then you become aware of adding to that physical sensation with the desire to get rid of it. Notice the actual sensation that you have in the body and the aversion to it, the desire to get rid of the pain. Notice that the breath doesn't arouse desire. Maybe you have a desire to concentrate your mind, to become one who has *samadhi* or something like that: 'I want to become a person who can attain *jhana*.'

But the actual breathing is neither attractive nor interesting nor unattractive. For most people, the idea of attaining *jhana* is attractive; to become somebody who can get *jhana* is attractive. So we can go about doing *anapanasati* with that desire; or maybe you have a distracted mind – the mind wanders, it doesn't do what you want. You want it concentrated on the breath, but every time you start it wanders off. And then you want to get rid of the distracted mind, you want to become someone who has a composed and concentrated mind, and not be someone who has a wandering, distracted mind. So there's *vibhava-tanha*, desire to get rid of the wandering, distracted mind by becoming somebody who has a concentrated mind and can attain *jhanas*.

This is a way of reflecting on desire. Desire for sense pleasure, desire to become, desire to get rid of. If we really contemplate and know *vedana* exactly through *vijja*, through mindfulness and wisdom, then we don't create desire. There's still the pleasure, the pain, the neither-pleasant-nor-painful, but things are as they are. This is the *suchness*, the way things are; it's the Dhamma, the Truth. So there's no suffering when things are as they are. Suffering is a result of desire-grasping-becoming (*tanha-upadana-bhava*). From there, the sequence of *paticcasamuppada* goes to birth, ageing, death, sorrow, lamentation, pain, grief and despair (*jati-jara-mananam-soka-parideva dukkha-domanassa-upayasa*). The whole sequence of misery follows from *tanha-upadana-bhava*.

So contemplate this theme of *paticcasamuppada* during this retreat. The desire to get rid of desire is still a trap of the mind, isn't it? Contemplation is not getting rid of, but understanding. This is the way of knowing, of *vijja* rather than *avijja*.

DEPENDENT ORIGINATION V:
LETTING GO OF DESIRE

The arising of *dukkha* is due to the grasping of desires. And the insight is that there is this origin or arising and that desire should be let go of. This is the Second Noble Truth; it is the insight knowledge of letting go.

Some people think that all I teach is 'whatever happens, let go.' But the teaching involves a real investigation of suffering: insight of letting go occurs through that understanding. So 'letting go' does not come from a desire to *get rid* of suffering – that is not 'letting go', is it?

The *vibhava-tanha* – or desire to get rid of – is quite subtle, but wanting to get rid of our defilements is another kind of desire. 'Letting go' is not a getting rid of or putting down with any aversion. 'Letting go' means to be able to be with what is displeasing without dwelling in aversion – because aversion is an attachment. If you have a lot of aversion, then you will still be attached. Fear, aversion – all this is grasping and clinging.

Dispassion is acceptance and awareness of things as they are, letting go of the aversion to what is ugly or unpleasant. So 'letting go' is not a trick phrase coined as a way of dismissing things, but it is a deep insight into the nature of things. 'Letting go' therefore is being able to bear with something unpleasant and not being caught up with anger and aversion. Dispassion is not depression.

How many of you dismiss and refuse to acknowledge the unpleasantness of the functions of your own bodies? There are certain functions of the human body that aren't beautiful, that in polite society we do not mention. We use all kinds of euphemisms and ways of politely excusing ourselves at the appropriate moment, because one does not want the perception of oneself to be connected to those functions. We want a presence or image to be connected with something pleasing or interesting or attractive. We want our photograph taken with flowers in an attractive setting, not on the toilet. We want to disguise the natural processes of life, cover up the wrinkles, dye the hair, do everything to make ourselves look younger – because ageing is not attractive.

As we get older, we lose what is beautiful and attractive. Our reflection is to be really aware of sickness and death, that which is attractive and unattractive: the way things are in this realm of sensory consciousness. Being an entity with sense organs which contact objects – which can be anything from the most beautiful and pleasing to the most hideous and ugly – we experience feelings. Feeling (*vedana*) entails the dualism of the pleasant, the painful and the neutral; this applies to all the senses – taste, touch, sight, hearing, smell and thought.

I use that particular word *vedana*,, that *khandha*, as the concept for all that attraction/repulsion. We are experiencing *vedana*, we are aware of the pleasant, painful, beautiful, ugly, neutral through the body or through what we hear, smell, taste, touch or think. Even memories can be attractive. We can have memories that are pleasing, unpleasant or neutral. And if we are heedless and operate from *avijja*, the view of self, the unquestioned assumption that 'I am' – the attractive, the unattractive and neutral is interpreted with desire. I want the beautiful, I want the pleasant, I want to be happy and successful. I want to be praised, I want to be appreciated, I want to be loved. I don't want to be persecuted, unhappy, sick, looked down on or criticised. I don't want ugly things around me. I don't want to look at the ugly, to be around the unpleasant.

Consider the functions of our body. We all know that these functions are just part of nature but we don't want to think of them as being *mine*. I have to urinate, but one would not want to be known in history as Sumedho the Urinator.' Sumedho the Abbot of Amaravati, that's all right.' When I write my autobiography, it will be filled with things like the fact that I was a disciple of Ajahn Chah, how sensitive I was as a little child, innocent and pure – maybe a little mischievous now and then because I don't want to be seen as a cupie doll. But in most biographies the unpleasant functions of the body are just dismissed. We are not to go round thinking we should *identify* with these functions but just begin to notice the tendency to not want to be bothered with them, or pay attention and observe a lot of that which is part of our life, the way things are.

In mindfulness then, we are opening our mind to this, to the whole of life, which includes the beautiful, the ugly, the pleasing, the painful and the neutral. So in our reflection on the *paticcasamuppada*, we see it is connected to the Second Noble Truth.

This is where the sequence *tanha-upadana-bhava* is most helpful as a means of investigating grasping.Grasping in this sense can mean grasping because of attraction or because of aversion, trying to get rid of. Grasping with aversion is pushing away; running away is *upadana*, as well as trying to get hold of the beautiful, and possess it and keep it, seeking after the desirable, trying to get rid of the undesirable.

The more we contemplate and investigate *upadana*, the more the insight arises: desire should be let go of. In the Second Noble Truth it is explained that suffering arises, it should be let go of and then, through the practice of letting go and the understanding of what letting go really is, we have the third insight into the Noble Truth: desire *has* been let go of: we actually know letting go. It is not a theoretical letting go, it is not a rejection of anything, it is the actual insight.

In discussing the Second Noble Truth, there are the statements: 'There is the origin of suffering', 'it should be let go of'; and the third insight: 'it has been let go of'. And that is what practice is all about – fulfilling those three.

That applies to each of the Noble Truths: there is the statement, what to do, then the result of that. The First Noble Truth: there is suffering; it should be understood; it has been understood. These are the three aspects of insight into the First Noble Truth. The Second Noble Truth: there is the origin of suffering, which is the grasping of desire; it should be let go of; it has been let go of. The Third Noble Truth: there is the cessation, *nirodha*; it should be realised; and the third insight: it has been realised. The Fourth Noble Truth: there is the Eightfold Path, the way out of suffering; it should be developed; it has been developed. This is insight knowledge.

When you think: 'What does an arahant know?' it is this: he knows there is suffering, he knows suffering should be understood, the arahant knows when suffering has been understood; the arahant knows the origin of suffering, he knows it should be let go of, knows that it has been let go of, etc. These are the twelve insights. This is what we call arahantship – the knowledge of one who has those insights.

Paticcasamuppada is a really close investigation of the whole process. Now it is grasping of the five *khandhas* that is the problem. The five *khandhas* are *dhammas** – they are to be studied and investigated. They are just the way things are. They are not self; they are impermanent. To know this, to know the way it is, is to know the Dhamma.

And so the grasping of the conditioned world as a self is based on delusion or ignorance (*avijja*): the illusion of a self as being the five *khandhas*. And because of that we live our lives based on ignorance. The volitional activities (*sankhara*) from that ignorance interpret everything with the 'I am' and from the grasping of desires; the result is *jara-marana* (ageing and death). If I grasp the body as self then 'I' get old. My body is 54 this year, it's sagging and wrinkly. And the belief that 'I am getting old' because the body is getting old is a kind of suffering, isn't it? If there is no sense of self, then there is no suffering. There is an appreciation of its ageing. There is no feeling that there is anything wrong with the body getting old; that is what it is supposed to do. That is its nature. It is not me. It is not mine, and it is doing what it is supposed to do. Perfect, isn't it? I would be upset if it started getting younger! Imagine if I started getting younger, fifty years from now I'd be back in nappies and I'd have to go through all that again.

The thought 'I am getting old' isn't sorrowful. It is a conventional way of talking about the body. But if this is what I think I am: 'I am the body, this is my body', then ignorance conditions *sankhara* and everything is coming from that ' I'm getting old, I want to be young, I want to live a long life, don't you call me an old man, you young whippersnapper !' Why? Because of the identity with the body.

I also reflect that I am going to die. 'That's a morbid thing, let's not even talk about death. Of course we are all going to die but that's far away.' When you are young, you think of death as so far away – 'let's enjoy life.' But when anyone we know dies, or we nearly die, then death can be very frightening. And all that is from the attachment to the identity with this body.

Then, of course, there are all the views, feelings, memories and biases we have (*vedana, sañña, sankhara*). Not only do we suffer from

---

*dhamma means 'thing' as part of the universe(i.e. not belonging to a person). Dhamma refers to the Buddha's teaching and insight into the Ultimate Truth.

identification with the body, but also when we attach to the beautiful and to feelings, 'I want only the beautiful, I want only the pleasant; I do not want to see the ugly; I want to have beautiful music and no ugly sounds, only the fragrant smells. . . .'

We attach to what the world *should* be like; opinions about Britain, France and the USA. Attachments to these views and opinions and perceptions make up the *vedana-sañña-sankhara* sequence of the five *khandhas*. And we can the attach to all that in terms of self. 'It's my view, what I think, and what I want and don't want, what should be and what should not be.' So we get grief, anguish, despair, depression, sorrow, lamentation from that illusion of self.

The insight into the Second Noble Truth is that there is an origin to this suffering. It is not permanent. It is not absolutely always that something arises. The rising up of *dukkha* is due to the grasping of desire. You can see desire because it is *dhamma*, it arises and ceases.

You can see the desire that arises to seek the beautiful and pleasant on the sensual plane through eyes, ears, nose, tongue, body and mind. *Kama-tanha* is sensual desire. Sensual desire always wants some kind of pleasurable or at least exciting experience. *Kama-tanha*: you can see it in the movement that we have of going towards and then grasping the sensory pleasures.

Bhava-tanha is the desire to become. This is to do with wanting to become something. Ultimately, since we do not know who we are, our desire is to attain and achieve and *become* something. In this Holy Life, the *bhava-tanha* can be very strong. You feel that you are here to *become* enlightened and achieve and attain something. It all sounds very good. But even the desire to become enlightened can come from this *avijja*, from this self-view. 'I'm going to get enlightened. I'm going to become the first American arahant; I'm fed up with this world, I want to get enlightened so that I will not have to be reborn again. I don't want to go through childhood again. I don't want any of that. I want to become something where you don't have to be born any more.' That can be *bhava-tanha/vibhava-tanha* – they go hand in hand. In order to become something you have to get rid of the things you don't like and you don't want. 'I'm going to get rid of my defilements and I want to get rid of my bad habits and get rid of my desires, – and all this sounds very righteous, too. The defilements are bad – get rid of them.

So in the Holy Life, there is a lot of *vibhava-tanha*. We can live this life solely to get rid of things and to become something by getting rid of something. Notice then that the Second Noble Truth is the realisation that desire should be let go of, should be laid down. It is not a rejection of desire but an understanding; you let it go. Because otherwise it is *vibhava-tanha*, the desire to get rid of desire. Know it, see it, but don't make anything out of it. If you are coming from ignorance, your desire says: 'I want to become an enlightened being and I shouldn't think like that, I shouldn't have the desire to become a Buddha; I shouldn't want to become anything.' All that can be from ignorance conditioning mental formations (*avijjapaccaya sankhara*). So then there is the insight knowledge: 'Desire should be let go of.'

All this sounds very right in a way when we say 'we shouldn't be attached to anything', but that can also be coming from *avijja-paccaya sankhara*. 'I shouldn't be attached to anything' is very much an affirmation of myself as somebody who is attached to something and shouldn't be that way. I should be otherwise. So that's just a trap of the mind, that's not a real insight into *kama-tanha, bhava-tanha, vibhava-tanha*. Reflect on what attachment is. If you are really just throwing things away, it is not the way to solve this problem, is it? You are not really examining *kama-tanha, bhava-tanha, vibhava-tanha*, so you won't have an insight into letting go. You will merely take a position against attachment, which is another kind of attachment.

So examine, look into attachment. This is working in a much more subtle and realistic way than just forming an opinion that you shouldn't be attached to anything.

I remember a psychiatrist who lived in Bangkok, who used to take somebody's wrist-watch. . . and they would get upset and he would say: 'You are attached to your wrist-watch.' Then he would take his own watch and throw it away to prove he was not attached. He was bragging about this to me. I said 'You have missed the point. You are attached to the view that you are not attached to your wrist-watch.' That isn't letting go, is it? Throwing this away like a smart alec and saying 'you are attached, I'm not, I threw mine away'. There is a lot of self in that? 'Look at me I'm not attached to these wretched material things.' You can be quite proud of being non-attached. With reflection we see attachment and we don't have to get rid of things, but we can not be attached to them, we can let go of

153

them – not by throwing them out, but by understanding the suffering that comes from being attached.

As you understand the peace of non-attachment, of letting go, the Second Noble Truth leads to the Third. When you let go of something, you are aware there is no attachment to the five *khandhas*. There is awareness that desire has been let go of. Then the insight into the Third Noble Truth of cessation arises. There is cessation. This cessation should be realised.

As we realise the cessation more and more, we begin to notice non-attachment. Not many of you are aware of non-attachment. You are usually conscious through being attached to things. A totally deluded human being only feels alive through attachment and desire. Contemplate that when you are not caught up in attachment to the five *khandhas*, you do not feel alive, you are nobody. Having neurotic problems makes people feel interesting and alive. 'I have fascinating neuroses from all kinds of traumas in early childhood.' So it's not Sumedho the Urinator, it's Sumedho the Interesting Neurotic, the Mystic or Sumedho the Abbot – these are conditions we can be attached to. Realising cessation allows you to let the self cease; there is letting go. The realisation of letting go is cessation, that whatever arises ceases. And cessation is noted. Cessation should be realised.

So our practise is one of *realising* cessation. That is when we talk about emptiness: we realise the empty mind where there is no self. There is no sense of the mind being anybody. As soon as you think of this as 'my' mind, if you grasp that thought, then you are deluded again. But even if you have 'my mind' and see it as that which arises and ceases with non-grasping of it, then it is just a condition. There is no suffering from that, it is peaceful.

When there is no self, there is peace. When there is 'me' and 'mine', then there is no peace. Worry, anxiety what are they? They are all from 'me' and 'mine.' When you let go, then there is cessation of 'me' and 'mine'. There is peace, calm, clarity, dispassion, emptiness.

I observe that when there is no self, no attachment, then the ways of relating to others is through *metta* (kindness), *karuna* (compassion), *mudita* (sympathetic joy), *upekkha* (serenity). These are not from a self or *avijja*. It is not that there's an idea that 'I must have more *metta* for everyone because I have a lot of aversion and I should not. I should have loving-kindness for all beings. I should feel compassion. Sometimes I just want to kill everybody. I should feel a lot of *metta, mudita*, be kind and joyful and sympathetic with people. I should be serene, too.' The *brahma-viharas**, as ideas for a selfish person, are not the real practice. The desire to become someone who has lots of *metta* and *karuna* and all that kind of thing is still *bhava-tanha*.

But as the illusions of self fall away, then this is the natural way to relate. You do not become a vacuous zombie through understanding Dhamma. You still relate to each other but it is through kindness, compassion, sympathetic joy and serenity, rather than through greed, hatred and delusion.

What do unselfish human beings, generally manifest in society? You could explain *metta, mudita, karuna* and *upekkha* as qualities which manifest through unselfish human beings. Then apply that to our own practice now. When there is *vijja* – knowing and seeing clearly – then that gives total opportunity for the practice of kindness, compassion and the rest. But it is not me, not mine; not Sumedho, the *metta*-filled Ajahn, Sumedho the Good Guy, rather than Sumedho the Urinator. As soon as Sumedho-delusions step aside and cease, kindness, compassion, sympathetic joy and serenity can manifest. This is why the human state is a great blessing: when the self-view is relinquished, what remains is a great blessing.

But it is not me. 'I' am not a great blessing. All I can do in this conventional self is to let go of delusion. To be mindful and not get attached to things, to see clearly – that is what I can do. That is the practice of the Four Noble Truths and development of the Eightfold Path. It amounts to that vigilant, mindful seeing of things clearly. Then what happens is up to other things. There is no need to go around trying to become 'Sumedho the Good Guy' any more. This goodness can manifest through this form if there is no delusion; and that is not a personal achievement on attainment at all, merely the way things are. The way it happens to be. It is Dhamma.

---

* The 'divine abodes' of kindness, compassion, sympathetic joy and serenity

THE
SHINING-THROUGH OF
THE DIVINE

What is divinity? We may consider ourselves as purely instinctual creatures, because we have an animal body with the same instinctual nature as an animal. Survival and procreation are just as strong in us as they are in cats, dogs and wolves. But also there is the divine. This is something that we rise up to or turn to; because it's not instinctual, it won't be something we'll find unless we deliberately seek it.

For reflection on divinity, we have the four *brahma-viharas*, the beautiful, selfless qualities that can manifest through the human form when there's no self. When you're not caught in instinctual behaviour or emotional reactions based on ignorance; when there's dispassion and all that process of self-view ceases, then the divinity is obvious. Then kindness, compassion, sympathetic joy and serenity of mind are not something that we have to get, but something that manifests through these forms.

In our lives as separate beings, we relate to things. As individual beings, we have relationship to things, we have to meet and contact and react or respond to objects all the time for the rest of our lives. On the physical level, we have to respond to each other's presence in some way, either ignoring or embracing or paying respects or cursing. In relationship, when there's no self, then there is this divinity that manifests. So you can see that the human form is a form for the divine.

On the other hand, we can think it's just for yourself, 'It's my life and I can do what I want, I have the right to happiness' – and all that kind of selfishness. On an instinctual level, if we don't rise above animality, we can just live very much following instinct or emotion or we can live in a world of ideas and attachment to ideas of how

157

things should be, which is very much a problem in the Western world. But as you penetrate that and see the suffering that comes from grasping anything at all, as that insight brings about the letting go and the non-attachment, then there's a response to the way things are which can be divided into these four categories of the *brahma-viharas*.

Metta, karuna, mudita, upekkha provide a reflection: they form a sequence of how to relate to the human realm, to the animal kingdom, and to nature. *Metta* is very much how we should relate to ourselves, too. It's how to relate to ourselves with kindness and acceptance rather than with aversion and judgement. *Metta* implies that we accept something that may not be very nice – like if you have physical pain or things that aren't very nice about your body or your character. Maybe you have a lot of fears or bad temper or something like that. If you have *metta*, it means you can accept these for what they are. You're not judging it or condemning it from an ignorant, self-conscious position. You're aware of it as painful, unpleasant or ugly – but *metta* practice is the ability to accept patiently the flaws, the pain, the irritations, and frustrations within our minds and bodies and the unpleasant and annoying things that impinge on them from outside.

This is because with *metta* such things are no longer seen as personal, there's not me and you, no 'You've done this to me . . .' or 'I've done this to you.' *Metta* is having perspective and not creating a problem even about the unfairness, injustice, inadequacies and so forth, of ourselves or others or of society. It doesn't mean that we don't notice or that we can't see; but it means we don't make problems about it, we don't carry it around in our minds with bitterness, resentment, anger and destructive tendencies. With *metta*, there's always the ability to forgive and start anew, to recognise the way things are and not expect everything to fit the ideals we have regarding how things should be. It doesn't mean that we fatalistically resign ourselves to mediocrity, tyranny and stupidity, but it means that we aren't caught in the pattern of ignorance conditioning mind formations. So we can bear with the vicissitudes of life with kindness and acceptance.

Then there's *karuna*. *Karuna* is compassion. When we see the suffering of others and the injustice and unfairness that exist, we respond with compassion, but it's not like a wealthy person feeling sorry for the poor; that's not it. It's not looking down on the poor, not patronising or feeling sorry for people, but it's understanding the predicament of our human condition and all that goes along with it. It's from understanding the nature of suffering, how it arises and ceases, that you can have true *karuna* for other beings.

The British have a lot of *karuna* for animals, don't they? Britain is quite an impressive country when you think how much wildlife there is in this densely populated area of Southern England. That's a good quality: *karuna*. So Britain is a kind country, where people generally have developed compassion – concern for the unfortunate and the underprivileged.

When we moved to Chithurst*, there were people who didn't want us there; but most of the local people were trying to be fair. They had compassion for us, in other words, a certain measure of compassion. They were not going to harm us or try to get rid of us even though they may have preferred a nice Christian monastery or nice, proper upper-class family to buy Chithurst House, a family who would raise horses and play polo. That would have been more with the general mood of West Sussex because people like what they're used to. But because there was *metta-karuna* already developed, there were only a few people that were directly hostile or would take any action against us. So one can regard this as *metta-karuna*.

Sometimes, in Theravada Buddhism, one gets the impression that you shouldn't enjoy beauty. If you see a beautiful flower, you should contemplate its decay; or if you see a beautiful woman, you should contemplate her as a rotting corpse. This has a certain value on one level but it's not a fixed position to take. It's not that we should feel compelled to reject beauty, and dwell on its impermanence and on how it changes to being not so beautiful – and then downright repulsive. That's a good reflection on *anicca*, *dukkha* and *anatta*; but it can leave the impression that beauty is only to be reflected on in terms of these three characteristics rather than in terms of the experience of beauty. This is the joy of *mudita* – being able to appreciate the beauty in the things around us.

Flowers are a lot prettier than we are; we admit they're prettier; we expect them to be; we don't envy them their beauty. But we might really hate somebody else for being beautiful because then it's a threat. Somebody else's beauty makes *me* look not so beautiful. That's

* The residence in West Sussex that became the first Buddhist forest monastery in Britain in 1979.

me, isn't it? This is to be observed; not to try and force a kind of false happiness onto the situation, but to let these things cease in your mind. To be clearly aware of this particular problem is to stay with it and not make a problem about it from self-view. Then recognise it as *anicca, dukkha, anatta*; let it cease; let go of it. Then, in that letting go, we find a rejoicing in the talents and the goodness and the beauty of other beings.

When you look at flowers, you experience a joyful feeling and that's *mudita* – you're rejoicing in or glad at the beauty of something. Maybe you've never reflected like that. We see beautiful things in nature, and, because they're no threat to us, we can rejoice in the sunset or the beauty of trees and mountains and rivers. So that's *mudita*: a rejoicing in beauty and goodness and truth. And we rejoice in the goodness of others. When somebody does something good, or you hear about some noble action, or some heroic effort, or some self-sacrifice, a sense of *mudita* arises. That's joy, sympathetic joy.

But where we tend to fall short of this is where it becomes a matter of 'you' and 'me.' We can be very jealous of somebody's health and beauty if we are caught in the self-view. We might feel joy at the flowers in the garden, but then we go to the neighbour's house and her flowers are more beautiful than ours. We might feel envy because from a self position it's: 'Her flowers look better than mine, and she is more beautiful than I am'; or: 'He is better looking than I am, he is more intelligent'; or: 'He has a better personality' – all this. So we suffer from this envy and jealousy. It's a very common problem; in fact, many human beings are really stuck in envy and jealousy.

If we were to go to a rich person's house with its beautiful grounds, the swimming pool, beautiful oriental carpets, lovely furnishings, the selfless person might rejoice at being in a beautiful place. One might also think: 'Hum, wealthy people probably got it from cheating the poor and ripping off the underprivileged. . . grumble, grumble, grumble.'

I remember going into a church one time with somebody in London and it was a beautiful church. I said, 'Oh, what a lovely church.' He said, 'Yeah, it was probably at the expense of all those colonies the British exploited.' I wasn't commenting on the history of the church, but really experiencing the gladness of being in a beautiful place. And yet we can think that maybe that church was built out of the slave trade or the opium trade. Perhaps slave traders and drug traffickers in the last century felt guilty, so they built a magnificent church in London. Yet that doesn't mean that it's not beautiful, does it? We're not judging it on the moral plane but reflecting on the joy, on the experience of beauty, goodness, and truth: these are what bring joy into our lives.

People that can't see the beauty of the good or the true are really bitter and mean at heart, ugly; they live in an ugly realm where there's no rejoicing in beauty and goodness and truth. To rejoice in these things doesn't mean that we get carried away with them; the experience of joy no longer occurs if we indulge in beauty and try to grasp it or if we hold on to the experience of joy to try to have it all the time. But *mudita* is certainly a part of our human experience.

Mudita is our ability to be joyful with the beauty and loveliness of life's experiences. It is the sense of joy and appreciation and gratitude for the beauties and the lovely things of life, and the lovely things in other people. So that when there's no self then there's joy; you find a joy in the goodness, the beauty of the people around us or in the society or the natural conditions. Once you have insight, then you find you enjoy and delight in the beauty and the goodness of things. Truth, beauty and goodness delight us; in them we find joy: that is *mudita*.

If you see beauty as something to grasp, then it arouses desire. You see beautiful human beings, a beautiful woman or man and you think: 'I want them.' That's desire. That's not rejoicing in the beauty of someone; it is the desire to possess, control and get something for yourself out of it.

On the level of instinct, that's the way it is. That's natural enough. If we didn't find each other attractive, no-one would want to procreate the species, would they? If sexual activities were painful and miserable, nobody would want to do it. And if we found each other totally repulsive and ugly, then we wouldn't want to get close to each other, not to mention anything as intimate as sex. Desire is the natural way on that level of the sensory realm. There's nothing wrong with it, but there is the possibility for the human being to transcend it. If desire was all we were and all we could do, then we should follow it. But because we can transcend, we have this connection to the divine, we can rise above the coarse, instinctual nature of our own bodies and the animal realm.

And that's what I'm pointing to; I'm not condemning the animal realm. Animals can bring us a lot of joy. Down at Chithurst recently, I spent the day with Doris, our cat, and I always felt her bring me a lot of joy. She's a very pleasant animal. If I get attached, however, I say: 'I've got to have Doris. I've got to bring Doris here to Amaravati. I can't live without her.' Then I drag her up here, and she would have to fight with the cats who live here and it's all just for me, just so I can get what I want. Then that wouldn't be a joyful experience any more. It would bring a lot of problems.

We can reflect on how things are affecting us. To always want *mudita* – the beautiful flowers, the waterfalls and the beautiful birds singing – means that you can't rejoice in them any more because you're trying to hold on. You're trapped in all kinds of views, opinions about it, so even if you're in the midst of it, you're not really enjoying it, rejoicing in it any more, because you've been separated from it through your desire for it.

In our life as *samanas**, contemplating nature, contemplating the Dhamma, we don't have to think that all beauty is just there to corrupt us and give us another rebirth. That's another self-view, isn't it? But be aware of how beauty affects you. When you see a beautiful woman or handsome man, how does it affect your mind? There may be the initial attraction and then one can easily get into feeling threatened and rejecting it because we have a life of celibacy. You might also give a second glance and dally with the sexual thoughts that might arise from that eye contact. However, the more you are mindful, the less you tend to follow things as desire, the less you tend to create or add to the feelings with desire and attachment.

So enlightenment doesn't mean a kind of bland indifference. Sometimes enlightenment is made to sound like we can become emotionless zombies, people that don't feel anything any more. Well, as long as there's self, then what we would call joy tends to be tinged with selfishness; it becomes stained with our selves. We get jealous if we have something beautiful and somebody has something more beautiful because selfishness always turns beauty into possessiveness, doesn't it? If the beauties of life – the joy of truth and beauty and goodness – come from self, then they're always corrupted with jealousy, envy and begrudging people.

When there's selfishness, even if you are the most beautiful of all, it's not really a joyful experience because you are always worried that there might be someone claiming that crown. If you adopt a

---

*samana means 'spiritual seeker', in this context one whose practice has taken them to the commitment to a religious form of life

162

self-view, there's always that possibility, isn't there? But when there's no self, then beauty doesn't belong to anyone. It's not mine or yours; we realise there's no possibility of possessing it anyway, so there's no desire to possess. There can be the joy of the experience of beauty without it being corrupted with selfishness.

Then *upekkha*: equanimity, serenity. To be able to abide in serenity of the mind, we're not going around looking for beautiful things to find delight in, because there's no self. You respond to beauty with joy but it's not something that you're looking for or seeking as a person any more. The ordinariness of life is *upekkha*, serenity. It's about having peacefulness with the pains and aches of the ageing process and the separation from the loved. All this is the realisation of *upekkha*, serenity.

Upekkha doesn't mean indifference. Sometimes it's translated as indifference but it actually means serenity when things are ugly or unpleasant or ordinary. If you follow the *asubha* practices – noticing, paying attention to that which is not beautiful – then you begin to create *upekkha*, equanimity or serenity.

There was a hospital in Bangkok that would get all the murders and violent deaths, corpses found in the canals and things like that. If you went in on a Monday, they would have a collection from the weekend and a variety of gruesome, macabre objects that would first give you a strong feeling of revulsion. You'd go in and say, 'Yuk! Let me out of here!' – because you don't generally like to look at human bodies that have been butchered and mangled and are in a state of decay. Civilised society always keeps away from such things. We have all the institutions to take care of that so that it never has to meet our attention.

But actually if one meditates on it, then the result is equanimity or serenity. If you get over the initial aversion and horror and negativity towards the human corpse that's rotting or been cut up in an autopsy, the result is equanimity or *upekkha*, tremendous peacefulness and serenity. Not depression. Not aversion. When there's no self, one can abide in a state of serenity. If there's self, then we say, 'I hate it, I don't like it, take it away, I can't stand it. I can't bear this. It's foul, it's disgusting. . . .' But when there is equanimity, *upekkha*, there is no self. So one is not making problems about the process of living and the way things move and change and go from beauty to decay. With *mudita*, you find joy with the beauty, and when the beauty fades, then there's equanimity rather than sorrow, serenity rather than sorrow and despair at the loss of the beauty.

Upekkha is the ability not to follow aversion and be carried away when you see beautiful things. So we're not just running around trying to rejoice in beauty or feel karuna for every unfortunate creature. We can allow the waiting when there's nothing much happening. With upekkha, one does not have to seek something to get happy about some cause to fight for, or get involved with compulsive activity. This is another great problem for modern humanity: we try to use up restless activity in good causes, because there's no upekkha.

Traditionally, the brahma-viharas are considered as lokiya dhamma, mundane Dhamma, not the transcendent or lokuttara dhamma. Because of the way the mind tends to think, the view arises that they're not worth bothering with. 'Lokuttara dhamma is the important one. You don't pay much attention to lokiya dhammas.'

But with mindfulness, you're with the relationship of the lokiya to the lokuttara dhamma. We relate on the lokiya dhamma level through the brahma-viharas – metta, karuna, mudita and upekkha. When there's no self, when there's no ignorance conditioning the mental formations, then there is the way of things – the lokiya dhammas. But we're not asking mudita to be a permanent experience. We're not expecting to have a continuous, absolute, eternal experience of rejoicing and joy in our lives because we're not attached to that as a viewpoint.

So the brahma-viharas represent a spontaneous response to this experience of birth and consciousness when there's no self. They're a spontaneous response from selflessness, from anatta, rather than an impulsive reaction from desire. There's a difference between a spontaneous response to wisdom and mindfulness and an impulsive reaction to desire. The difference lies in that view of a self. In the self-view, one is still grasping, just reacting impulsively with desire to life's impingements and experiences. When there's no more ignorance, then there's spontaneity.

That's what spontaneity is. There's no self in it. It's just a more and more natural way to respond to beauty, truth and virtue; or to pain and misery; or to winter, spring, summer and autumn; to the fortunate beings or the unfortunate ones; and even to the waiting, holding your cup of tea, looking out of the window at the rain.

This is just a contemplation of what divinity is. If you reflect on the instinctual nature, the earth-bound body, its sexual desires, the procreative abilities, survival, eating, drinking, sleeping, all these basic instinctual necessities, there's nothing bad about them; it's just the way a form like this survives. It has to procreate itself, doesn't it? In fact, human beings are getting too good at procreating themselves. It's rather frightening, isn't it? How many billions is the world population? Four or five billion on this planet? And if they were all just like animals, just operating out of instinct, that is four or five billion selfish, undeveloped, neurotic, screwed-up human beings. Terribly frightening, isn't it? We can take it to the opposite extreme – five billion enlightened human beings! Now that might not be so bad! Five billion enlightened human beings rather than five billion ignorant, selfish human beings. Five billion human beings who can manifest the divine in their daily lives, through *metta*, *karuna*, *mudita*, *upekkha*. That doesn't sound so bad, does it? Sounds rather nice.

But five billion human beings manifesting greed, hatred and delusion is a pretty grim picture. Yet we don't have the right to comment on *them*: this one here, this is what we have, this is what we can work on. Don't worry about the others. This one here is what you can actually develop through reflection and through meditation.

A TIME TO LOVE

With the emphasis Buddhists place on reflection, mindfulness and wisdom, the Holy Life might sometimes seem to be an almost unfeeling attempt to look at everything in very objective ways. Rather than feel things, we're supposed to see everything as *anicca, dukkha,* and *anatta.* That's how it might seem. But remember, the heartfelt experience of life is a loving one so that love and devotion are not to be dismissed.

If we're looking at the experience of love as just *anicca, dukkha,* and *anatta,* that might seem cold-hearted. Objectivity, however, is merely the way of having things in perspective so that love is not something that blinds us. If we're attached to the idea of love, then we can be quite blind to its reality. We can get very inspired by talking about it or meditating on love – seeking it in others, demanding it or feeling somehow left out. But what is love in terms of our lives as we live them?

On an emotional plane you might want to have feelings of tremendous one-ness, or maybe aim the feelings at some particular person, wanting to have a special, loving relationship with another person. Love can also be abstract – love of all human beings, love of all beings, love of God, love of something or of some concept.

Devotion is from the heart, it's not a rational thing. You can't make yourself feel love or devotion just because you like the idea of it. It's when you're not attached, when your heart is open, receptive and free, that you begin to experience what pure love is. Loving-kindness, compassion, sympathetic joy, equanimity – the realm of the Divine Abodes, the *brahma-viharas* – these come from an empty mind. Not from a sterile position of just annihilating feeling but from a heart that is not deluded, not blinded by ideas of self or others, or by passions of some kind or another.

You may think the Holy Life is cold and heartless because, in a community of *samanas* such as this, living according to a way of restraint and discipline, we're not demonstrative in our expressions of love and joy. This community is not bubbling up with feelings of devotion. It is quite formal and restrained in its form and its expression. But then this does not necessarily deny love. With mindfulness, with the way we relate – to our own bodies, to the Sangha, to the lay people, to the tradition, and to the society – there is an openness, kindness and receptivity. There is caring, a joyfulness and compassion that we can feel.

It is still *anicca* and *anatta*, and it is *dukkha* in the sense that it's not in itself the end of anything; it's not satisfying as an identity or an attachment. But when the heart is free from illusions of self, then there arises a loving quality in the pure joy of being. It's not expected to be anything or anybody; neither is it expected to last or be permanent. It is not to be made anything of. It's just the natural way of things. So when you contemplate in that way, that is the way of faith and trust and devotion.

When we talk about faith and confidence and trust, they're nothing you can really grasp. Faith is not anything that you can create. One can say the words, but to really have faith and confidence in Dhamma is to be willing to let go of any demand or affirmation or any attachment whatsoever. And that experience of faith comes to us as we examine and understand the Dhamma, or the true way of things. If we really contemplate Dhamma, see Dhamma, then there is faith, this strong sense of total trust, confidence in truth.

If you're practising *vipassana* meditation and you're getting more frightened, anxious or tense, or feeling emotionally sterilised, then you're not doing it the right way. Perhaps you are using technique as a way of suppressing your feelings or denying things. So you end up feeling more tense, sceptical, uncertain. There is an attachment to some view about it. The more we *really* see and understand completely the way things are, the more we have this quality of faith. This faith increases, it's a total trust. When one talks about surrender or giving up or letting go, it's through total trust. It is not just taking a chance or a risk, it is through the experience of faith.

The path is something we cultivate. We have to know where we are and not try to become something that we think we would like to be; we have to practise with the way it is now, without making a judgement about it. If you're feeling tense, nervous, disillusioned, disappointed about yourself or the tradition, or the teacher or the monks or nuns, or whatever, then try to recognise that what is in the moment is enough. Be willing to just admit, to acknowledge the way it is rather than to indulge in believing that what you're feeling is somehow an accurate description of reality or that it's wrong and you shouldn't be feeling like that. Those are two extremes. But the cultivation of the Way is to recognise that whatever is subject to arising is subject to ceasing. And this isn't a put-down or cold-hearted way of cultivating the path, even though it might sound like it.

You might think you just have to let go of all your feelings and see that the love in your heart is *anicca*, *dukkha*, *anatta*. You feel love for the Buddha and you think, ' Oh, that's just *anicca*, *dukkha*, *anatta*. That's all it is!' You feel love for the teacher and you think 'That's just *anicca*, *dukkha*, *anatta*. Don't get attached to the teacher!' You feel love for the tradition. . . '*anicca*, *dukkha*, *anatta*, don't get attached to traditions, – or techniques.'

Not getting attached to *anything* can merely be a way of suppressing *everything*. It's not necessarily letting go or non-attachment, it can merely be a position you take. And if you take that position and you operate from that position, all you're going to feel is negativity and stress. 'You shouldn't be attached to anything; you shouldn't love anything, you shouldn't feel anything – feeling anything is just *anicca*, *dukkha*, *anatta*.' That means you're just taking the words and you're using it like a bludgeon, a big club to your mind. You're not reflecting, opening and trusting.

Metta practice is one of the beautiful devotional practices that is highly recommended in Buddha-Dhamma. Loving-kindness. As human beings we're warm-blooded creatures. We do feel love. That is part of our humanity. We like each other; we like to be with people; we like to be kind; we get enjoyment out of cooking food and giving it to other people. We enjoy helping. You can see that with the custom of *dana* in the Asian communities. When Sri Lankan people come here with their curries, they light up. It is the joy of giving.

Now that's a very good quality, isn't it? It's beautiful to see somebody who may have been up all night preparing delicious food to offer to somebody else – they're not cooking it for themselves. Well, what is that as a human experience? Is it defilement or is it being attached to the delight or happiness of doing things for others?

This is the beauty of humanity, isn't it – just being able to love, to give, to share, to be generous.

Try contemplating what would be the great delight of being the richest person in the world? What would be the truly delightful thing? To get what I want? No, it would be the opportunity to give it away, wouldn't it? That would be the true delight of being rich and wealthy – so that you could give it away, as *dana*, generosity; whereas to be rich and not to be able to give it away would be a real burden. What a burden that would be, to be the richest man in the world and be selfish and hold onto it and keep it all to myself. The joy of wealth is in one's ability to share it and give it without any kind of corrupt intentions or selfish demands.

So this is what is lovely about our humanity: we can experience this joy of giving. And it's something we all experience when we really give something, when we help somebody without any selfish request or demand for something back. Then we experience joy. It is certainly a lovely human experience – but we don't expect it to make us joyful for the rest of our lives.

The joy of generosity and kindness isn't permanent, doesn't make us permanently happy – but we don't expect it to. If we did, it wouldn't be *dana* any longer, it would be a deal we were making. It wouldn't be an act of generosity, it would be buying something.

Real joy comes from giving and not caring about whether anyone even knows or acknowledges it. As soon as the self comes in, for example: 'I'm giving this *dana* to you and it is very important that you know who's giving this *dana* – ME, I'm giving it!', then the amount of joy that comes from giving is probably very minimal. If I'm so concerned that you recognise and appreciate my generosity and my goodness, then that becomes a joyless state of mind. One cannot feel happy or have real joyfulness in living if there is attachment to the idea that one's actions should be recognised. There's nothing wrong with people appreciating somebody else's goodness and generosity – but when we don't demand it, then there is joy.

Romantic love is usually based on the illusion of a self and a demand for something back. Spiritual love, then, is altruistic love or universal love and is represented by the *brahma-viharas* – *metta*, *karuna*, *mudita* and *upekkha*. Such love is a unitive experience. It brings together, it unites. It is a communion. Hatred is the experience of separation. When we hate then there's no union, communion or oneness. Hatred is separative, divisive, and discriminative. Love is unitive and we want unity because living in a world of hate, discrimination and separation is a miserable hell-realm.

The community is a communion, a Sangha, a whole. If we're divorced from the Sangha, if we hate the Sangha, 'Hate this nun, hate that monk – and I don't like that, don't like this,' then this is not community, it's a dis-unity. That feeling is one of alienation, separation, emphasising me and you, *your* faults and *my* feelings, and my anger at your faults. It can also be my emphasising the things that are wrong with you – things that are wrong with the monks, things that are wrong with the nuns, things that are wrong with the anagarikas, things that are wrong, full stop. And attaching to those perceptions will make me feel alienated, separated, angry, discontented and depressed.

Sometimes the mind will go into a very negative state where all you feel is annoyance. Whatever people do doesn't seem quite good enough. When you're in that mood, then everything seems wrong – the cats, the sun, the moon – the mind goes into division, separation, and negativity. You feel separate from everything you see, and no communion or union is possible as long as *you* are identified and attached to that attitude of mind. When you are in a loving mood, then it doesn't really matter whether somebody isn't feeling very good or they're not doing exactly what they should. There are always little things, little bits and pieces that aren't quite what they should be. But when you're in a loving mood these things aren't so important.

So the loving experience comes because you're willing to overlook the personality differences and the discrimination that exists in the conditioned realm for the feeling of communion, of union, of oneness. We are uniting as brothers and sisters in a common experience of old age, sickness and death rather than pointing out the differences or who's better than whom.

When we take refuge in Sangha, we're taking refuge in *supatipanno* (those who have practised well), *ujupatipanno* (those who have practised directly), *ñayapatipanno* (those who have practised insightfully), *samicipatipanno** (those who practise with integrity). Rather than taking refuge in Americans, British, Australians or in men or

---

*These terms form part of the daily chanting in honour of Buddha, Dhamma, and Sangha

women or in nuns or monks, we take refuge in those who practise the Dhamma – in the good, the direct, the sincere.

We have tendencies for both union and for separation and we can be mindfully aware of these. The way things are has to be recognised as Dhamma. There is uniting and there is separating, and with clear awareness one is not identifying with either extreme. There's time for union and communion; time for non-discrimination, for devotion, for gratitude, for generosity, for joy.

But there's also time for separation and discrimination for examining what's wrong. There is a need to look at the flaws – to look at anger, jealousy and fear – and to accept and understand those emotional experiences rather than judge them and take them as self and as something that you shouldn't have. This is what being human is all about: we're born into a separate form and yet we can unite. We can realise unity, community and oneness; but we can also discriminate.

So the refuge in the Buddha is the ability of a human being to recognise both sides, and to respond appropriately. We can look at the flaws and the problems of life as part of our human experience rather than in a personal way. We are no longer proliferating, nor are we magnifying or exalting, obsessed with what's wrong because we have this perspective of unity and separation. This is the way things are, the Dhamma.

Is being a Buddhist monk or a Buddhist nun a denial of love? Is the Vinaya discipline merely a means of suppressing feelings? It *can* be just that. We *can* use Vinaya discipline and monastic tradition as merely a way of avoiding things. Maybe the monks are just frightened of women. . . . Maybe the nuns are just petrified of men so they become nuns and they don't have to face their fears and anxieties with regard to relationships with men. . . And, of course, many worldly people think like that, don't they? They think we're all here because of an inability to cope with the real world.

But is that really how it is? If it is, if that's what you're a monk or nun for, then you're in it for the wrong reasons. This is not an instrument for avoiding reality and life but for reflecting on it. Because in the restraint and in the dignity of restraint, the way of monasticism is an expression of love for *all* beings – men, women, both inside and outside. We're now no longer choosing one person to focus our attention on and devote ourselves to, but we devote ourselves to all beings.

I realise if I were a family man, my whole attention would have to be towards my wife, my children and immediate family. That's the result of family life and what marriage is about. They have priority. You have to relate with regard to those who you are married to and responsible for.

One can be an alms-mendicant, live on faith alone, on the trust in the goodness and benevolence of other beings because one feels love or respect for all beings. Love and respect for all beings is what generates the alms that sustains us in this life as alms-mendicants.

And the funny thing is that the power of the Buddhist Sangha is so strong that even if you personally hate all other beings, the alms still come in! The power of the robe seems to be so strong that even if you as an individual monk or nun hate everybody, you're still going to get fed by kind-hearted beings. This is because of the *paramitas* of the Buddha. This doesn't mean you should develop hatred or justify it in yourself in any way. Rather, it's a reflection on the power of a very skilful convention that was established by the Lord Buddha. When you appreciate that, then you really feel love and trust.

Why do these monasteries here in England work? Why should they work in a non-Buddhist country? Why should anybody want to send a cheque by mail, bring a sack of potatoes or prepare a meal? Why should they bother? This is because of the *paramitas* of the Buddha. The goodness of the lifestyle he established generates generosity. The loving-kindness, the compassion and joy of the Holy Life reaches out and opens other people to that same experience.

It is a mystery. From a practical, worldly attitude of justifying our existence in the eyes of society, we don't look like we do all that much for anyone. Many people think we just sit here and try to get enlightened for ourselves – have nice, pleasant mental states because we can't stand the real world. But the more you contemplate this life and understand it, the more you realise the power of the goodness, the faith, the *paramitas* of the Buddha which allow a communion to take place in an inter-connection of goodness.

And it needn't be demonstrated, talked about and emphasised a lot. It speaks for itself. We don't have to go out telling people: 'You should give us alms because we are practising the Dhamma and we are disciples of the Buddha.' Our requisites are offered because people appreciate and respect the Holy Life. It brings joy and happiness into people's lives because we rejoice in the beauty of others and in the goodness and benevolence of this experience of living.

Actually the Holy Life is a strange one, a strange way to live. Quite how it works is a mystery in terms of what we regard as reality according to our cultural conditioning. But as Dhamma, as Truth, as the way things are, it actually works. And this increases our faith, and our trust in the Refuges and in the beauty and goodness of our lives as *samanas*.

Reflections on Benevolence

May I abide in well-being,
in freedom from affliction,
in freedom from hostility,
in freedom from ill-will,
in freedom from anxiety,
and may I maintain well-being in myself.

May everyone abide in well-being,
in freedom from hostility,
in freedom from ill-will,
in freedom from anxiety,
and may they maintain well-being in themselves.

May all beings be released from all suffering
and may they not be parted from
the good fortune they have attained.

When they act upon intention
all beings are the owners of their action,
and inherit its results.
Their future is born from such action,
companion to such action,
and its results will be their home.
All actions with intention,
be they skilful or harmful;
of such acts, they will be the heirs.